WITHDRAWN

BEEN THERE, DONE THAT

GROSSET & DUNLAP

An Imprint of Penguin Random House

EDITED BY MIKE WINCHELL

Been There, Done That

WRITING STORIES FROM REAL LIFE

FOR
ANNE SCHMIDT
THE INSPIRATION BEHIND COUNTLESS
WORDS AND STORIES

GROSSET & DUNLAP

Penguin Young Readers Group
An Imprint of Penguin Random House LLC

Collection copyright © 2015 by Mike Winchell. Cover illustration
copyright © 2015 by Eglantine Ceulemans. All rights reserved.
Published by Grosset & Dunlap, an imprint of Penguin Random House LLC,
345 Hudson Street, New York, New York 10014. GROSSET & DUNLAP is
a trademark of Penguin Random House LLC. Printed in the USA.

Library of Congress Cataloging-in-Publication Data is available.

ISBN 978-0-448-48672-7   10 9 8 7 6 5 4 3 2 1

CONTENTS

Sacrifice

PUTTING OTHERS FIRST

Why or Why Not?

ASKING QUESTIONS ABOUT THE WORLD AROUND YOU

Things Will Never Be the Same

DEALING WITH CHANGE

Foreword

Mike Winchell

f you were to ask a group of authors for advice on what to write about, I'd bet most would tell you to "write what you know" and use real events and people from your life in your stories. But there would also be some authors who would say you should "just write." Yet even these authors would probably agree that real experiences can be used as seeds that can be planted to help create a story. Once you've experienced something, it's a whole lot easier to write about it. I know this because I always take my real-life experiences and spin them into stories somehow.

For example, when I was five years old, my parents had just gotten divorced, my older brothers loved picking on me, and I was about to start school. So yeah, things weren't going too well for me. Luckily, my first trip to Disney World was coming up, and with all the drama in my five-year-old life, the "Most Magical Place on Earth" was sure to cheer me up. Right?

Wrong.

I lost my Mickey Mouse wallet—given to me by my father when we'd first arrived at the park—and he decided he'd teach me a "life lesson" by not giving me another wallet or any more money for the rest of the trip. My brothers taunted me with their wallets and money for the next few days, I cried nonstop, and the end result was that I hated the mere thought of Disney from that point on.

But when I got older, I realized that the "wallet at Disney incident" wasn't *all* bad. It taught me a couple things that made me a better person later in life. First, it showed me how tough divorce is on a kid, which led me to vow to get married only if I was one hundred percent sure. Second, I learned that kids—like my own children—deserve a second chance before giving a harsh "life lesson" that might scar them emotionally.

More importantly, even though it wasn't a happy time, losing my wallet at Disney helped me as a writer because it inspired me to write a short story about a boy who goes to an amusement park and finds a wallet with a magical ride pass inside. A pass that grants him access to secret rides no one else can see. I took that true experience of losing my wallet, and then spun it around to create a pretty cool story.

And there it is—the motivation behind putting together this anthology: *Been There, Done That*. For this book, each author selected an experience that dealt with a family member or friend, and then used it to inspire an original work of fiction. Sometimes the made-up story is very close to the actual experience. Other times, only hints of the true experience are present. Regardless, what follows are examples of how your favorite authors have not only gotten through these experiences, but have used them to create stories.

Happy reading,
Mike Winchell
Editor

Mike Winchell

FOLLOW THE LEADER?

The Push and Pull of Peer Pressure

It's tough sometimes, figuring out when you should listen to your friends and follow their lead, and when you should ignore them and head off in your own direction.

Authors Gary D. Schmidt, Caroline Starr Rose, Alan Lawrence Sitomer, and Claire Legrand all examine how peer pressure can sometimes push kids to do things they might not normally do.

LOVE, LIKE LEECHES...

Probably the best job I ever had—the best job I ever will have—was a job at a summer camp on the maintenance crew. I had to deal with plugged up toilets and corn dogs and kids who threw up—mostly because of corn dogs—but I also built a new cabin and messed around in boats that needed repair and put in docks and planted gardens and built rock walls and assembled bonfires and did a whole lot of things I could never do in the suburbs of New York City. And when I wasn't doing any of those things, I'd play baseball near high pines and swim in clear pools that emptied out in small waterfalls and lay down in the middle of a field to watch hawks circle on the thermals above.

I lived for those summers in the Catskill Mountains. When high school was what high school often is, filled with jerks and would-be jerks and locker rooms and meaningless home-work and drama about not very much and social status crap, I thought of that camp, those mountains, and the friends I had up there who loved what I loved and still love: high grass and hawks on thermals and mountain pools and pines.

And camp had one other thing, the most important thing, the really, really most important thing: Mindy White. Mindy White had long dark hair. She had green eyes. When she laughed, her voice was like Poetry. When she smiled, her smile was like Beauty. When she looked at me, I wished more than anything that she loved me like I loved her.

But she didn't. Because Mindy White was actually in love with another guy at the camp, a little older than me, who was an idiot. I tried telling Mindy White that Lee Buttface was an idiot, but she was too much in love. She talked about Lee while I did the dishes. She talked about Lee while I helped her peel the carrots. She talked about Lee while I fetched cabbages from the basement below the kitchen, or the lemon pies from the freezer, or the canned ravioli from the pantry. She talked about Lee while I scraped the burned oil and lard from the grill in the kitchen—the hottest and most awful job at camp, but one I took my time on, because she worked beside me. I scraped the grill with my shirt off—it was that hot—and I thought that might do something. It didn't. She loved Lee Buttface.

For two years I listened to Mindy White talk about Lee Buttface, until I heard one day over the winter that Lee Buttface had broken things off—I told you he was an idiot. I was over-joyed. I was thrilled. I was filled with fathomless hope.

I went to the weight machine and began a program of lifting.

The next summer, Mindy White came to camp. Lee Buttface, too. And you know what? She still loved him. Really. She still loved the idiot. Even when he started going with someone else at camp. Even when I stood over the grill, shirtless and buff and everything, she still loved the idiot. She read me stories she had written, and in every story, the hero's name was . . . well, do I even have to say it?

There was a set of falls near the camp. It was filled with black and leechy water. We swam there anyway, mostly because of the jumps—even though you had to puck the leeches off your skin every time you came out of the water. You could jump into the big pool at the bottom from a rock about twelve feet up. But you could climb to the top of the falls and jump into the small pool that gathered there from forty feet up. And that pool really was no bigger than your outstretched arms. No kidding.

One day I went there with two of the counselors—and Lee Buttface, who didn't know that I hated him. The whole way there, Lee Buttface told us how he was going to jump in first, how he wasn't afraid of any heights, how he figured he was going to *dive* in headfirst, how he had done stuff like this plenty of times.

When we finally stood on the ledge in brutal sunlight, the two counselors jumped, then I jumped, and then Lee Buttface stood alone and looked down. And looked down. And looked down. I have to say, I felt sorry for him. I could see he was about to wet his pants. But he looked down, and he looked down, and he looked down, and finally I called up and told him to climb back, he didn't need to jump, it was fine, we'd come and do it another day, it was really fine.

He climbed down.

The whole way home, he explained why he hadn't jumped. The water was filled with leeches, he said. He was allergic to leeches, he said. He could die from leeches, he said.

I wanted to tell Mindy White he'd chickened out. I really wanted to tell Mindy White he'd chickened out. But I never did. The next day in the kitchen, she read another one of her stories about wonderful, marvelous, amazing Lee, how he saved the day, how he was loving and kind and true and blue.

I kept my shirt on, and scraped the lard from the grill.

FALLS

The best job, I mean, the really best job at any summer camp is maintenance—because after you've finished scraping corn dogs and baked beans off two hundred plates and after you've wiped corn dogs and baked beans off twenty tables and after you've swept corn dogs and baked beans off the floors beneath the twenty tables—which isn't easy—you're free until suppertime, when you have to set the two hundred plates on the twenty tables again. So you can hike to the falls below Napanoch Road, which I had never seen but which were supposed to be seventy feet high, and where once two kids got caught in the undercurrent beneath the falls and didn't show up again until the next spring.

I could hardly wait to see them.

The falls, I mean.

And it's where I was heading right now, along with Mark Mann and two other guys who I didn't really know from farms down the road.

But not with Mindy White—who I really wanted to swim at the falls with.

She wasn't coming.

Did I say that I really wanted to swim at the falls with Mindy White?

Did I say that I had been in love with Mindy White since Camp Orientation?

She waved as the four of us left. I waved back, even though I was pretty sure she didn't know my name. She had green eyes and long black hair. How could I not have waved back?

But she wasn't coming with us, and instead I was walking to the falls with Mark and these two other guys who had the arms and chests that throwing cows and hay bales around will give you, I guess.

The July sun was brutal, and we took off our shirts and draped them over our backs, and our sneakers sank into the asphalt of Napanoch Road, and Mark said he could hardly wait to get under the water, and I said I could hardly wait, either. So when we climbed over the guardrail and down the bank into the cool of the hemlocks, I was ready to dive beneath the falls—who cared about undercurrents? I was really ready. And I could hear them, hidden as they were behind the trees, pouring gorgeous white water over the high rocks, cascading into a crystal pool speckled with sunlight, the cool mists coating the green and mossy shores, the pine boughs, the rocks, and soon, me.

We slid down the last of the path—the pine needles were

slick — and came into the white sunlight below the falls. I looked up at seven stories of water gushing down. At seven stories of dirty dark yellow water gushing down.

Dirty dark yellow water gushing down into a black and eerily still pool.

No cool mists coating anything. Nothing green and mossy. Just stony shores crusted with — something.

Did I say the water was black?

It really was. I shoved a pine branch beneath its surface. It disappeared.

"We're not going to swim in this," I said.

Mark looked at me like I was crazy.

"Of course not." He pointed up the falls. "We have to climb to the top."

I looked at him like *he* was crazy.

Seventy feet high. The water spraying over the rocks — which looked pretty slimy. Gray plant stuff on most of them — and it looked pretty slimy, too. And did I say seventy feet?

"To the top?" I asked.

He nodded, and together with the other two guys, we skirted the black pool, leaning against the rock walls so we didn't touch the water, and reached the bottom of the falls.

Just for the record, the rocks *were* pretty slimy. They even smelled slimy. And they were sharp.

Mark left his shirt on a rock — we did, too — and he began to climb beside the cascading yellow water. We did, too. "Don't look down," he said, and he laughed like it was so funny. I guess

8

the other two guys thought it was so funny, too, because they laughed just like Mark did.

I didn't laugh.

Everyone always says, "Don't look down." But of course you look down. Of course you do. You want to see the sharp rocks you're going to hit after you slip off that first hold. So I looked down as I heaved myself up, one ledge after another, leaving the sharp rocks farther and farther and farther beneath me so that the impact when I hit them would be greater and greater and greater.

"You all right?" hollered one of the guys beneath me.

He probably figured I was going to take both of them with me when I slipped.

"Never better," I hollered back.

Translation: *This is how people die.*

But since I'm telling you this, you know that I didn't, and that I clambered up behind Mark when we reached the top, and that I looked down again at the whole slimy seventy feet and tried not to upchuck.

While the other two guys clambered up, Mark showed me another pool, close by a shadowed cliff. This pool was tiny. If you were floating in it right now, you could stretch out your hands and touch both sides, easy. But you wouldn't want to float in it, because the water was black here, too.

"That?" I asked Mark. "We're going to swim in that?"

He said something, but the sounds of the waterfall bounced off the slimy rocks and filled the air and I couldn't hear him at all.

He pointed, and I looked up.

"There's a ledge above us," he screamed.

"So?"

He moved his hands up and down as if he were pulling himself up.

I got it: more climbing.

And the rocks were slimy and sharp again. Of course.

We climbed — Mark, then the two guys, then me. Forty more feet, the thunder of the waterfall in our ears, me looking down the whole time.

I didn't fall. I didn't upchuck. I didn't wet my shorts — which is why the two guys went ahead of me, because they thought I might. We climbed, and climbed, and finally clambered up to a ledge where nothing was slimy because we were so far above the water, but where we still had to be careful because the ledge was pretty thin and four of us were standing on it.

I looked down. The dark pool was the size of a quarter.

"What are we doing up here?" I asked.

"We're going to jump," Mark said.

I looked over the ledge again.

"What?" I asked.

"We're going to jump."

"Where?"

"Into the pool," he said.

I pointed down. "That pool?"

"You see any other?" He kicked his shoes off. So did the other two guys.

Right then, I think I hated them all.

"That pool is tiny," I said.

"Yeah. So be careful you don't miss."

"You going to wet your shorts?" said one of the other guys—which was good timing because, in fact, I thought I might this time.

And then I got it. I finally got it. No human being would jump into a tiny pool from forty feet up. Especially a tiny pool with black water. No one would be that stupid. This was a test. This was three guys from farms testing me, the city kid from New York, who lived where no two trees touched their branches together. It was all a joke. All a stupid joke.

"All right," I said. "So where are we really going to swim?"

Mark smiled and stepped to the edge. He looked back at me, turned, put his leg out, and fell.

I thought he was dead.

I really thought he was dead.

Did I say I thought he was dead?

I looked over the edge. He wasn't dead. He was just climbing out of the pool and quickly wiping himself down—I wasn't sure why—and now he was looking up and grinning.

"You coming?" he hollered. I could just hear him above the sound of the falls.

I'm not sure I was glad he wasn't dead.

The other guys stepped to the edge. They looked back at me, smiled, turned, put a leg out, and fell, one after the other.

I guess you can figure out how that left me alone up on the ledge.

I looked down. All three guys were standing on rocks above the pool, still wiping themselves as they looked up at me. "You coming?" they hollered.

Of course I was coming. I mean, what would you do?

I stood at the edge, toes clenched around the rock. This wasn't something you could practice. If you jumped out too far or to the sides, you'd miss the pool, hit sharp rocks, and die. If you didn't jump out far enough, you'd scrape against the sharp rocks all the way down and leave whole organs hanging behind you. After that, the current coming across the pool would wash your organless body over the seventy foot cliff and down to the undercurrent below—and they wouldn't find you until next spring.

"You coming or not?"

Did I say that I hated them?

I flexed my knees. I was going to do this. I bounced up and down a little. I really was going to do this. I flexed my knees again. I'd have to be sure not to scream on the way down. I flexed my knees again. I really, really was going to do this.

I looked down at the tiny black pool.

Flexed my knees again.

Looked down at the tiny black pool again.

And . . . I wasn't going to do this.

Would you? I hardly even knew two of these guys, and I had only known Mark for two or three weeks. At the end of the summer, I'd be going home, where no one jumped off ledges into black pools. I'd probably never see these guys again. So if

I didn't jump, so what? My dog would still love me. None of my friends would ever hear about it. The sun would come up tomorrow morning. So what?

I took a step back.

And that's when Mindy White showed up.

Mindy White. Did I tell you she has green eyes? Long black hair?

She clambered up the rocks and called to the guys and her long black hair blew behind her, and Mark pointed up and Mindy White turned her green eyes to me and she said, "Is Ethan going to jump?"

That's what she said: "Is Ethan going to jump?"

And suddenly, the world was clear, because I knew two things. First, Mindy White knew my name. (Did you catch that?) Second, I was going to jump.

I stepped to the edge. I clenched my toes. Flexed my knees. A little more bouncing. Remember not to scream on the way down. Another bounce.

And I stepped out.

I took about half an hour to fall those forty feet. I watched the black water coming closer and closer. I didn't scream. I kept my arms at my sides so I wouldn't snap off my fingers by hitting them against the rocks. I blew out my nose so water wouldn't get forced up into my brain. And then I was under.

Under!

Alive!

Okay!

Under, Alive, and Okay! And Mindy White had seen me jump!

Back to the surface.

It was beautiful. Everything was beautiful. I climbed onto the rocks. I looked down at the pool, and then at myself, and I knew right away why the water was black: It was filled with leeches. As fast as I could, I wiped them off and pucked the ones who had gotten hold, but I didn't even care. It was all beautiful. The sharp and slimy rocks. The black pool. The leeches. The white and brutal light. It was all beautiful. Because Mindy White — who knew my name — had watched me jump with her lovely green eyes.

And I let my eyes move up to her, because she was standing on the rocks above the pool, and her black hair was blowing, and there she was.

Kissing Mark Mann.

Kissing Mark Mann.

Kissing Mark Mann.

There she was.

Later, we climbed down the rocks beside the seventy-foot falls. The two guys first, then Mark and Mindy, then me.

I never looked down.

Caroline Starr Rose

LITTLE NIPPERS

n fifth grade, my mother and her friend wrote to a local radio station to receive ID cards sponsored by RCA Victor, the second-oldest recording company in the United States. While other kids used their IDs to join a club hosted by the station, these two had other plans. They started their own club, the Little Nippers, which they named for RCA Victor's company mascot, a Jack Russell terrier named Nipper.

The Little Nippers grew to include fourteen spirited, bright, opinionated girls. They met every Wednesday in a lavish backyard clubhouse. Being a Nipper was serious business. Parents knew not to schedule doctor's appointments on Nipper days. Girls knew skipping a meeting meant they risked being "bawled out" for the offense.

Every six weeks, the girls voted for new officers. The president was in charge of running weekly meetings, with the vice president serving as her assistant. The secretary kept minutes of each meeting, first in a school notebook and later in leather-bound journals. The historian gathered pictures, newspaper clippings, and other memorabilia for the Nipper scrapbook and was also in charge of "Love"—a separate scrapbook where she pasted comic strips, added lots of hearts to each frame, and changed all names to Nippers and their current crushes. The final officer was the sergeant at arms. She collected weekly dues—twenty-five cents from each member—and charged tardy members ten cents every time they were late. Her most challenging role was keeping order during meetings. Often she had to remove members who were arguing or goofing off, yelling or crying. Those thrown out of meetings were fined twenty-five cents.

The Nippers were well-read. One of their favorite activities was acting out the book *Little Women*, and every girl fought to play Beth March, the character bedridden with scarlet fever. The girl who landed the coveted role moaned on a couch and if she felt up to it, could hobble around on an old crutch kept in the corner of the clubhouse.

Each year the Little Nippers hosted elaborate Christmas parties for their parents, complete with handmade invitations and special musical and theatrical performances. They raised money through garage sales and Easter egg campaigns, volunteering their mothers to purchase the eggs and pooling all profits to pay for a week at summer camp. They played an awful game called Lemon Squeeze, where each person wrote an anonymous suggestion about how other members might "improve" themselves. This game often ended in tears, but they never stopped playing. They spoke a secret language called Carney (also known as

Kisarnisy), which they refused to teach their siblings but made a point to speak around them as often as they could. They spent nights at countless sleepovers and marched through their neighborhoods in slumber-party pajama parades.

THE LITTLE NIPPERS WHILE IN HIGH SCHOOL

The summer after ninth grade, the Little Nippers disbanded. The girls were about to enter high school and wanted to be open to new friends. But they never really followed through. Though official meetings ended, the Nippers continued to spend time exclusively with one another.

The Nippers grew up, married, had babies, held jobs. They became teachers and doctors, homemakers and CEOs. Now in their seventies, they gather for an annual reunion and act as silly as they did as girls.

When I was young, I loved listening to Nipper stories. The idea of a successful club run entirely without adults felt like every kid's dream. I was also drawn to them because of the girls' ingenuity—the way they planned things and made those things happen, the way their creative play and projects built one upon the other. But one of my favorite things about Nipper stories was the fact they always held an edge. The girls weren't always nice. Their strong personalities made conflicts inevitable and stories juicy, while somehow elevating loyalty above anything else.

THE STORY

LEMON SQUEEZE

ELENI SOTIS

Already we'd eaten soggy pizza,
opened my birthday presents,
spread out our sleeping bags in neat columns,
slipped into fuzzy slippers.

"I have a game we all can play.
It's called a Lemon Squeeze."
Friski wrinkled her nose.
"Squeezing lemons is not a game."

"Haven't you ever heard
'When life hands you lemons, make lemonade'?
That's what a Squeeze is all about:
learning bad stuff about ourselves and fixing it."

"That doesn't sound fun," Rachel whispered,
twisting a blond strand of hair
around and around her finger.

"It's a great way for friends to help each other out.
Last summer at camp,
there was a girl in my cabin
who picked her nose,
and I'm telling you, she quit
as soon as
we had a Lemon Squeeze."

Rachel twisted her hair
tighter and tighter.

I should have stopped there,
let the idea go.
But I was president,
and even at a slumber party
I got to be in charge.

"Write down each person's flaws
on these strips of paper.
Keep it
short
and
anonymous."

RACHEL CLAUSSEN

I was always so careful
not to draw attention,

and now

Eleni

wanted everyone

to write down

what they didn't like

about me?

Eleni gave my shoulder a playful shove.

"At least you don't pick your nose, Rach."

Big deal,

I wanted to say.

FRISKI CHEN

Each of us had a pile of papers,

secret messages scrawled inside.

It couldn't be so bad, right?

"I'll go first!" I said.

I opened a paper,

TOO ANNOYING

"Annoying?

Whoever wrote that

is just jealous of my talents!"

I jumped to my feet.

My legs starting kicking

in a fancy can-can,
my hands flashed,
my hips shimmied—
all my best moves.

reached down for another,
    A SHOW OFF

What did they know?
My dance routine
was good!
The best!

scooped up the next,
    SQUEAKY VOICE

"What's that supposed to mean?"
I tried to hold back,
but the words came out extra high.

The four girls
sitting cross-legged nearby,
nobody said a word.

the last.
    PANTS WAY TOO SHORT

"I can't help it if I'm growing
and my pants are like that.
Did you write that one,
Shorty Sotis?"

"Wasn't me," Eleni said.

"Your voice does get kind of squawky
when you get excited," Rachel said,
"but it's cute that way."

Like that was supposed
to make me feel better.

"Thanks a lot."
I pushed out of the circle
and slammed onto the couch.

"I'm done
with your
dumb
game."

NATALIE STATON

I unfolded the papers,
my fingers shaking.

SHY

TOO PRETTY

TOO WIMPY

NO BACKBONE

"See? Not too hard," Eleni said.

"She's not a wimp!"
Friski shouted from the couch.

I bit my lips, said nothing.

ELENI SOTIS

"I'll go next."
I spread the slips of paper
in front of me.

TOO BOSSY

NEVER WRONG—HOW'S THAT POSSIBLE?

GOSSIPS ABOUT "FRIENDS"

TOO SHORT

"How's that feel, Shorty?" Friski sang.

"Doesn't bother me."
I tried to make
my face
match
my words.

Lara pointed at Friski.
"For someone who's not playing,
you sure are yapping a lot."

"Don't talk like that to me!
Sarge!" Friski motioned to Rachel.
"Kick this girl out.
She's bugging me."

Lara rolled her eyes.

I wanted to step in,
say something,
but
I kept my
BOSSY words
to myself.

RACHEL CLAUSSEN

I had to get
the whole thing
over with.

TOO QUIET
the first paper said,

A PUSHOVER

CAN'T EVER DISAGREE WITH HER "BEST
FRIEND," ELENI

BLUSHES EASILY

Everything,
every humiliating thing—
the things I knew should embarrass me,
the things I had never even thought of before—
I had announced to the whole room.

If I didn't blink for at least a minute,
maybe the tears wouldn't slip
from the corners of my eyes.

Eleni touched my knee.
"You okay?"

"I don't think you're too quiet," Natalie said.

Great.
Straight

from the girl
who never had anything
to say.

"Blushing looks good on blond girls," Lara said.
"You don't get all tomato-y like I do."

Like that made me feel better.

I should have refused to play this game.
I should have told Eleni no.
But I'm
a pushover
who's never learned
to stand up for myself.

LARA ABRAMS

I was the last to go
    HUFFY
and took my time
    A BRAGGER
unfolding each bit
    TOO LOUD
of helpful advice.
    A KNOW-IT-ALL

"You've got to be kidding me!"

"Wait a sec," Friski said.
"Maybe I shouldn't yap,
but you do act
like you know a lot."

    I stuck my face in Friski's—
"I don't want to hear it from you."

    spun around—
"And the word is braggart,
by the way."

      yanked my sleeping bag from the floor
      and stormed from the room.

Rachel laughed,
but there was no happiness in the sound.
"Looks like you got your way, Friski.
Lara's kicked herself out."

ELENI SOTIS

We just sat there,
staring after Lara.

"It's been a long night," I finally said.
"I wouldn't mind getting some sleep."

"Shouldn't we go check on her?" Natalie asked.

I shook my head.
"Let's give her some space."
Without speaking,
everyone moved their sleeping bags
to separate corners of the room.

Stupid Squeeze.
Someone turned out the lights.

Stupid Squeeze.
I stared at the sagging crepe paper decorations
dangling from the chandelier above my head.

Wasn't a Lemon Squeeze
supposed to end in lemonade—
good things coming out of bad?

Everything
was a mess
and it was my fault.

All because
of that stupid
Squeeze.

WHAT REALLY HAPPENED

THE DAY I DITCHED SCHOOL

Yo, wanna ditch today?" Geoffrey Peterson asked me. "We'll blow this place and head to my house. It'll be cool."

Geoff asked me this question at 7:28 a.m. Come 7:30 the bell would ring and then adults from all over would start rushing us to class. It was a now-or-never decision.

"Sure," I said. I'd never ditched before. Sounded like fun. As we snuck away from campus I heard the school bell ring in the background behind me. Whether I was there or not, it seemed the day would go on.

We walked twenty minutes to Geoff's. "My mom's at work," he said as he turned the key. "She won't be home till 'bout four thirty."

"Cool," I answered.

First thing we did was eat. But Geoff didn't really have any good food. There were no frozen pizzas or microwave burritos, just cereal, but his mom was out of milk. I thought about pouring water on some Froot Loops but that seemed gross, so I simply decided to snack on some fat-free tortilla chips. That's the only thing Geoff had that I thought I'd like, a two-pound bag of fat-free tortilla chips.

We turned on the TV. I never realized how many dumb shows were on in the morning. Fat women talking about their problems. Skinny women talking about their problems. Lots of shows about lots of women talking about their problems. Finally we decided to watch a program where old people played price games to try and win a washer/dryer. *Dumb!* I looked at the clock. It was only 8:53 a.m. and already I was bored. Since I never got home from school until 3:15 p.m., I still had more than six hours to go before I could leave. We decided to play video games.

Geoff had weak vids though, stuff I had played over and over again about a hundred million times. After two and a half hours I was bored again. And hungry, too. But not really that hungry, 'cause it seems I had eaten about a pound of fat-free tortilla chips since I cranked open the bag. A gross, nasty taste sat on my tongue. Wow, could I have used a Pepsi. But Geoff didn't have any Pepsi, just water and ketchup.

I thought about leaving, but where was I to go? Back to school? No, I'd get in trouble. To the park? No, we could get caught by someone. To a friend's house? No, all my friends were at school.

I was SO bored.

The only excitement in the next few hours came when the mailman showed up. Geoff and I hid behind the couch thinking he might try to bust us or something, but he never even looked in the window. He just dropped off some letters and left.

When three o'clock finally came I opened the front door and felt the sun for the first time that day. I had a headache and wanted to throw up. It was like I'd been trapped in a shoe box all day, and holy smokes, did I need my toothbrush. I left.

"How was school, honey?" my mom asked when I walked in the door.

For a moment I panicked. I thought it was a trick question.

"Fine," I said nervously waiting for her to explode with rage.

"That's nice," she answered.

Turns out it wasn't a trick question. My mom never knew the difference.

The next day I found out our science teacher, Mr. Roddy, had brought a live tarantula to class and let it walk across his face. And Mrs. Ingram, the math teacher, broke her heel and fell down in front of everyone. Plus, I got an F on a pop quiz for history I totally would have aced, and I didn't get to see Amanda Byrnes, a girl I had a huge crush on, all day. Big bummer.

Then the kicker of all kickers came. I had written a creative writing assignment for English class. It was fun to write and funny to read and had a lot of laughs. Not only did I get an A on the assignment, but it was so good that my English teacher, Mr. Thompson, decided to read it aloud.

Not just to my class, but to ALL of his classes. The entire eighth grade!

So where was I during my moment of fame and celebrity and

awesomeness? Trapped without food in a land of weak video games, watching the seconds slowly tick by on a torturous clock.

Sure, the next day people congratulated me and told me they liked my story, but I totally missed The Big Day. It would be like winning the Super Bowl on Sunday afternoon, but not finding out till Monday that you were victorious, long after everyone had partied through the night. By the time I had learned of the news it was old news.

In a word: anticlimactic.

Later that week, when I saw Geoff at 7:28 a.m., I hustled into class before he could make eye contact with me. Maybe breaking the rules and being bad wasn't all it was hyped up to be.

And I never ate fat-free tortilla chips again.

WANDA PANSUCKLE:
THE WORST BABYSITTER EVER!

Cruel. Vicious. Has no right to be around kids whatsoever, much less babysit them.

Of course I am speaking about Wanda Pansuckle. This loony, nutty, totally coconuts woman who nearly ruined my life!

I could tell you about the three yellow warts on her nose. I could explain about her green breath. I could go on and on about how she had claws instead of fingernails, razor blades for teeth, and webbed feet.

None of it would be true. Wanda Pansuckle appeared to be as polite, nice, and normal as any regular ol' lady could be. That's what made her so sinister. What she looked like on the outside and how she actually acted were totally opposite.

"Hello, I'm Wanda Pansuckle. Quite pleased to make your acquaintance."

Those were the lines this six-hundred-year-old woman used to fool my parents into hiring her. Mom won a trip to Europe in a contest through our local supermarket and Dad refused, as he clearly said, "to take our son, Benjamin, out of school." Not that I was disappointed, because traveling with people who were actually excited to walk through museums and go gaga over portraits painted by dead people sounded like the boringest vacation ever offered to a kid.

I didn't want to travel for a gagillion hours on an airplane, I didn't want to eat food from menus written in languages I couldn't read, and I didn't want to stare at buildings and pretend that roofs and doors and window frames hammered together five hundred years ago captivated my interest.

And my parents didn't want to travel with a nonstop complainer.

So we struck a deal. They would go away and someone would stay with me for a week.

Of course whoever it was would have to be responsible, they would have to make sure I took care of all my responsibilities, and they would have to make absolutely certain I did everything my parents would have expected me to do.

Let's just say, it didn't quite work out that way.

On Day One, Wanda Pansuckle let me go to school with chocolate on my face. After letting me eat chocolate-chip cookies covered in double fudge chocolate sauce dunked in chocolate milk for breakfast. I didn't need to gobble any fruit, I wasn't required to brush my teeth before I left the house, and I didn't even have to wear clean clothes or comb my hair.

She just let me do whatever I wanted. And when I came home, it was more of the same.

I didn't have to do my homework. I didn't have to clean up my plate. I didn't have to turn off the TV, stop playing video games, or go to bed on time.

She let me do anything.

"This babysitter is weird," I told Mikey Lumpkin as we chatted in the school cafeteria on the second day of this. Mikey's lunch consisted of a turkey sandwich, a sliced apple, an organic fig bar, and a few non-fried sesame crisps. My bag, packed by me of course, contained powdered doughnuts, salty potato chips, a pickle, and a warm can of soda pop. "Like, I don't think she has rules whatsoever."

"Dude, you are the luckiest kid alive," Mikey told me. "You gotta push this babysitter to the limit. See how far you can go."

I plunked the tip of a can of whipped cream into my mouth and filled my face with a glob of white fluff. (Yeah, I brought that, too.)

"Ya think?"

"Absolutely," Mikey said. "Find this woman's limits."

"Wanna come over?"

"Can't," Mikey said. "My parents know your parents are out of town and they already told me I shouldn't even bother to ask."

"Bummer," I said. "But at least you'll know that this lady, Miss Wanda Pansuckle, is about to meet her *D-O-O-O-O-M!*"

"Awesome, Benny. And remember, you're not just doing this for yourself," Mikey said. "You're doing this for all kids everywhere."

I spent the rest of the afternoon making plans. Wanda Pansuckle had no idea what kind of ride she was in for.

When I walked in the house after school, Wanda Pansuckle passed me the phone. "Oh, Benjamin, it's your parents."

I covered the speaker with my hand.

"Should I tell them everything is okay?"

"Tell them whatever you want."

Was this a trick? I looked around the house. Dirty dishes in the sink. Clothes scattered everywhere. I'd forgotten to feed the dog.

Things were not okay. Not at all. But that's not what I told my father.

"Hi, Dad, how's your trip? . . . Yeah, yeah, things are fine . . . Sure, sure, I am being a good listener . . . Of course, I am keeping up with school . . . yep . . . Hi, Mom, how's your trip? . . . Yeah, yeah, things are fine . . . Yes, Mom, I am being a good listener . . . Very clean . . . Not up too late at all . . . Yep, limiting the TV . . . Pepper's great . . . Okay, speak to you tomorrow . . . Love you, too. Bye."

I hung up and realized I'd just told my parents more lies in one phone call than I ever told them in the entire history of my life.

What was this Wanda Pansuckle woman doing to me? I passed her the phone.

"I'm sorry, did you want to talk to them again?" I asked.

"No."

"You know," I said. "To, uh, fill them in?"

"Nope."

"Well, I guess you want me to go do my homework right now?"

37

"If you think."

"Or maybe clean up some of the mess I made last night or go feed Pepper or something?"

Wanda Pansuckle sat down on the couch and opened a book. "Up to you."

I squinted. This was very suspicious.

That's when I had my *Aha* moment! *Oh, I get it . . . she's testing me.*

Well, let's just see how she likes this. I raced to the kitchen and grabbed a piece of silverware from the drawer.

"Is it okay if I put this steak knife into the electrical socket?"

I put the tip of the blade right next to the wall outlet. Wanda Pansuckle casually looked up from her novel.

"If that's what you'd like to do."

I edged the steel tip closer. I wasn't even supposed to handle these kinds of super-sharp knives, much less go anywhere near electrocuting myself.

"I'm gonna do it," I said.

"Okay."

"I really am," I told her. "On the count of three I am going to jam it in there. One . . ."

She licked her finger and turned a page.

"Two . . . ," I warned, moving the silver tip right up next to the plug.

"Two and a half . . . ," I said real slowly. Wanda Pansuckle didn't budge. "THREE!" I yelled and tensed up all my muscles.

Wanda Pansuckle scratched her ear and continued reading

her novel, relaxed and at ease. I put the knife down.

This woman is an absolute loon, I thought. Time to take this to the next level.

Playing with matches!

I settled on a lighter when I couldn't find any matches. "Is it okay if I set the curtains on fire?" I asked with a click of the lighter.

I brought the orange flame oh-so-close to my mother's favorite drapes. Wall to ceiling, the material extended at least twelve feet, and for sure this kind of fabric had to be flammable.

"If that's what you want to do this afternoon, Benjamin, sure."

"Hello. Excuse me. I am, like, playing with fire right now."

"Do you need some help?"

"Help?" I said, flabbergasted. "You're supposed to stop me from . . . OUCH!"

The heat from the flame burned my finger, and I decided to go put the lighter back in the kitchen drawer before I really did something stupid to hurt myself.

This woman was clearly using psychology on me. Maybe reverse psychology. Maybe even reverse reverse psychology, the kind they use in the CIA, and at the movie theater to try to get you to buy the overpriced popcorn with a large drink in the combo deal that's never worth it. I fed the dog and loaded the dishwasher. I needed a new plan.

"So where are we?" Mikey asked the next day.

"Well," I said, popping a chunk of apple in my mouth for lunch. Last night I'd eaten candy for dinner. So much of it that before I went to bed I did one of those wet burps that gurgled up a small puddle of vomit in the back of my throat. After four days, taking a break from junk food wasn't an option; it was a necessity. "The situation is not looking good. I'm losing the battle."

"Take it to the next level, buddy."

"The next level? What's that?"

"An R-rated movie."

I gasped. "An R-rated movie? No way!" Then I thought about it. "Mikey, you're a genius!"

I'd never seen an R-rated movie before, and I knew that if I chose something super scary with lots of blood and guts and murder and death, then Wanda Pansuckle would come to her senses, turn off the movie, and I'd have my first victory in the war to get her to act like a proper caregiver and make me behave.

I entered the house and asked, "Can we watch a movie together?"

"Sure, Benjamin."

"But I want to watch something scary," I said, giggling to myself.

"Okay."

"Something R-rated. Like REALLY R-rated."

"That's fine. What's the name of it?"

I paused. I didn't know any R-rated movies. *Hmm.* I felt stumped.

"Want me to pick it?" Wanda Pansuckle offered.

"YEAH!" I said emphatically. "But make sure it's absolutely terrifying."

"You got it," she said. "Should I start it now?"

"Naw, let's watch it after the sun goes down. Scary movies are always better when it's dark."

"I agree," she said.

I went to my room, ditched my homework for the fourth day in a row, a new record for me, and eagerly counted the minutes until the sun sank over the horizon.

At 9:00 p.m. when it was good and black out, I went down-stairs. But not before turning off every light in the house. That'll get her, I thought.

"Ready?" Wanda Pansuckle asked.

"Ready," I said, stuffing a grape in my mouth. The thought of popcorn made me want to barf.

Three minutes into the movie I saw a dead person's head spin around. Fifteen minutes later I realized the dead person whose head had just spun around wasn't really dead, and was outside of a two-story house that looked kind of like mine. And he was about to cut off the pinkie toes of a bunch of giggling teenagers after having escaped from an insane asylum. Twenty minutes after that, the bad guy with the spinning head who'd escaped from the insane asylum, had not only chopped off eleven different pinkie toes, but he'd eaten eight of them and was wearing three others on a necklace. Next plan for him had something to do with chewing off a kitten's ear.

I couldn't let Wanda see, but I needed to get away from this movie. Far away. And I would have, too, but all the lights were turned off and I was too scared to walk through the dark house all the way to my room unescorted.

Wanda Pansuckle suddenly jumped. "Did you hear something?"

"Huh? What? Where?"

"Oh, nothing," she said relaxing back against the couch. "Thought I heard a squeak coming from upstairs."

A squeak, I thought. The head-spinning, pinkie toe–eater who escaped from the insane asylum had an artificial leg made of rusty metal that squeaked.

"I'm getting a little tired," I said, faking a yawn. "Maybe we ought to call it a night?"

"Don't you want to watch the end of the film?"

"Ya know, it's not really all that exciting," I lied.

Wanda Pansuckle reached for the remote. "It's one of my favorites, because usually the bad guy dies at the end of the movie, but in this movie the bad guy lives."

"Lives?" I said.

"Well, sure," Wanda Pansuckle replied. "It's based on a true story. Ya can't just change things like that."

A true story? Gulp. I reached down and touched my pinkie toe just to make sure it was still there.

"Well good night, Benjamin." Wanda Pansuckle headed off to the guest bedroom. Which, of course, was downstairs.

"So if you were too scared to walk to your room, where did you sleep?" Mikey asked me the next day when I told him all about the movie.

"On the couch with paper towels for a blanket."

"What'd ya use for a pillow?"

"My shoe."

"Ooh, rough. You were that scared, huh?"

"I told ya, this Wanda Pansuckle woman is crazy."

"You still have time to beat her," Mikey assured me.

"I dunno," I said.

"I do," Mikey exclaimed. "And you must. I have the answer."

"Oh yeah? What's that?"

He looked around to make sure no one else was listening.

"Cigarettes." Mikey rubbed his hands together and cackled. "You'll smoke an entire pack."

I wrinkled my nose.

"You'll get her to take you to the store, buy you a pack of smokes, bring you home, and then light you up. After you puff the first, you go for a second. After you finish a second, you go for a third. And then," Mikey said, completely in love with this idea, "you go into your parents' bedroom and you smoke three more butts. The smell will never come out by the time they get home tomorrow, and they'll freak out ten thousand percent. This, my friend, is a guaranteed win."

He smiled, big and proud.

"So let me get this straight. You want me to get cancer?"

Mikey didn't answer.

"And you want me to choke? Also, you want me to smell like an ashtray, pollute my lungs, foul up my parents' whole house, and inhale an entire pack of the worst substance a kid could ever put into his body? You know what the real problem is, Mikey? The real problem is that I've been listening to you!"

I stormed out of the cafeteria, and when I got home I did a week's worth of homework in one night in order to turn it all in for at least some sort of school credit. And then I did two loads of laundry, washed all the dishes, mopped the kitchen floor, bathed the dog, and even scrubbed the toilets.

Gross, right? Well, not to me. For dinner I had a fresh green salad, for breakfast I ate a scrambled egg, and for lunch I packed my own turkey sandwich with a side of sliced apple and an organic fig bar.

Which I ate far, far, far away from Mikey Lumpkin.

When I got home, my parents were just arriving back from Europe.

"Benny!" they exclaimed as we shared lots of hugs. After kisses, gifts, and me offering to help them bring their luggage in, both my mom and dad looked around at the house in amazement.

"Goodness gracious, this place is clean. Thank you, Wanda."

"Wasn't me," Wanda Pansuckle said. "It was all Benjamin."

"Benny!?" they squealed at the same time. Mom and Dad looked at one another in shock.

"I don't believe it."

"What's your secret?" they asked her.

"Secret? There's no secret." Wanda Pansuckle picked up her suitcase and got ready to leave. "Really, I didn't do anything at all."

She then walked out the door and left. *Thank goodness*, I thought. *Spending a week with Wanda Pansuckle was absolutely terrifying.*

Claire Legrand

THE BATTLE OF THE AXE

The roar of the crowds and the shouts of coaches running last-minute drills echoed throughout the concrete tunnel. Ahead of us stretched one hundred yards of immaculate green football field, grander than any awards show red carpet.

I flexed my gloved fingers and turned to the rest of the marching band. Lined up behind me in columns of crisp black-and-white uniforms, my fellow band members looked as excited and nervous as I felt—but I knew we'd be able to focus once it came time to perform. Instead of playing at our home field that night, we were at Texas Stadium, home of the Dallas Cowboys. Nothing less than that would have sufficed for that particular game—the countless rows of blue seats, the towering gray ceiling. Practically the entire populations of Lewisville and Flower Mound had made the trek.

Because that night, after all, was the Battle of the Axe.

Every year, about mid-season, Lewisville High School played our rival Marcus High School in the Battle of the Axe. The winner took home the Axe itself—a fairly ordinary-looking, wooden-handled axe, not impressive enough on its own to warrant all the fuss. I'm still not sure how the tradition started, but regardless, the game was one of the most important of the season—in some ways, even more so than the playoff games.

Our band director, Dr. Courtney, hovered nearby with his walkie-talkie. At his signal, I'd call the band to attention, and we'd begin our march-in, winding around the perimeter of the football field while playing our school's fight song.

I remember the weeks that led up to that battle. The annual Battle of the Axe was always a big deal, but it had been especially so that year. Our team hadn't been playing well, and there had been a lot of pressure on them to win at least this one, crucial game.

Two of the trombonists were trying to get the attention of the Farmerettes, our all-girl drill team, who stood lined up beside us. From out in the stands—on the Marcus side—came a low chanting. I had to listen hard to make out the words. Unsurprisingly, they were about how bad the Lewisville team was, and how we were definitely not taking home the Axe that night.

The words they used to express these sentiments were . . . not nice.

"Just focus on the show," I'd had to tell the band a few times that night. "The best thing we can do is give them the best show we can."

Tensions were always high around Axe time. Kids played practical jokes on people they knew at the opposing school—things like egging the other quarterback's house, for example. The morning before the game, at early practice, we band kids had noticed that someone from Marcus had placed a bunch of plastic cups in our school's chain-link fence.

The cups had been arranged to spell out vulgar anti-Lewisville jokes.

That kind of thing was harmless, though. The meaner pranks were what made me nervous. One of our cheerleaders got his tires slashed, so our cheerleaders retaliated, and a couple of kids from each school ended up getting arrested.

And then there had been the people on the highway that night, speeding by one another with their windows down, yelling out insults and throwing trash, their cars painted with pro-Lewisville or pro-Marcus messages. We band kids had seen everything happening from inside our buses. With all that swerving and honking, I had seriously thought someone was going to get hurt.

Dr. Courtney turned to me. It was time.

I called the band to attention with four loud claps. "Band, ten-hut!"

"Hut!" they replied in unison, snapping up their horns. They stood tall, their eyes sharp with determination. Our drum captain tapped off the rhythm. I took my position at the front of the band, my chin up in the air, and we marched onto the field.

With the red Marcus fans on one side of the stadium, and the maroon Lewisville fans on the other, separated by only a few empty rows of seats, the scene almost looked like two armies going to war.

I mean, I knew it was just a game; I wasn't naïve enough to think the game was anything like *actual* war. But I'd seen the slashed tires and the nasty graffiti; I heard the Marcus fans chanting and the Lewisville fans responding in kind. I hadn't been in the parking lot for the big fight the morning of the game, but I had heard enough to know it got pretty rough.

How many of those people throwing eggs and punches had been friends even a month ago? How many of them let something as silly as a football game ruin relationships and create trouble when there was no real reason for it? We all went to the same restaurants, the same mall, the same movie theaters; we were very alike, at our cores.

But because of this one tradition and this entirely ordinary axe, we'd started to turn against one another.

Our drumline continued playing as we took our seats, their mallets pounding a warlike rhythm into my skin. On the field, the football players stretched. A couple of them looked up at the screaming crowds and bowed their heads to pray. The stands around me that night were a sea of rhythmic clapping, face paint, and sweat.

Everyone's eyes were glued to the field.

Then, with a howl of sound from the fans, the game began.

This was it, what both towns had been preparing for the last few weeks. The game was brutal; both teams slammed into each other, merciless. Players committed penalty after penalty, and the shrill shriek of referee whistles pierced the air, louder even than the band as we performed "Celebration" and "Jungle

Boogie." I stood to the side, conducting the band through each song. They were so caught up in the game's frantic energy that they kept wanting to rush the tempo.

In the third quarter, a burst of shouting distracted me—a group of Marcus fans, their faces painted red and black, had come over from the Marcus side to tease the Lewisville fans. They held up rude signs and cheered along with our cheerleaders, but instead of cheering *for* Lewisville, they modified the cheers to insult our team.

A few Lewisville kids broke away from their group and lunged at the Marcus kids, their painted faces screwed up with anger. Some of the adults nearby tried to pull them away from one another; some adults joined the fight instead of stopping it.

Security guards in dark clothes showed up to defuse the fight. Once the kids backed up and calmed down, I noticed how they looked like kids again—sixteen and seventeen years old, just like me and my friends. They certainly didn't look like warriors once the fight ended, but for a moment, as they had snarled and punched and clawed at each other . . .

I remember not recognizing them as my peers in that moment. They had seemed to morph into something else. Something darker. With the kids escorted out, things in the stands returned to normal. Before too long, we were playing "The Hey Song" and cheering on the team like nothing had ever happened.

We ended up losing the game, 52–7. Our side of the stadium fell silent, while Marcus's fans erupted in cheers and taunts. The

Lewisville fans filed out into the parking lot in a fog of numb disbelief; my fellow band members kept dissecting certain pivotal plays from the game. What could the team have done differently? What mistakes had they made?

All I could think about, though, was that fight in the stands. The pounding of the drums. The hisses and boos undulating like toxic waves through the stadium. I knew we would all go back to our homes and our beds that night. We would mourn the loss and vow to win next year, to reclaim the Axe. Lewisville and Flower Mound would go back to being two normal Texas towns—not towns at war.

But I remember wondering, as I helped get the band back on our buses, if we would see the same kind of violence next year, the same darkness and anger roiling beneath the surface of everyone's cheers. I wondered if something truly horrible would happen someday, something worse than a fight in the stands and kids playing mean tricks.

I wondered, if that night had been a *real* war, if anyone would have been able to explain how it began.

THE VISITORS

T he Visitors came to the river town every year, on the longest day, at midnight.

They came wearing masks carved out of pale wood and tattered robes that smelled of smoke and sat thickly on their overlarge frames. They kept to the shadows as best they could, darting with broken screams through patches of light they could not avoid. They knew what would happen when they reached the gates, but they lurched toward them, anyway.

Some of them thought that beyond the river town lay their true home, from which they had long been separated.

Some of them thought that the world was shrinking, and this was one of the only safe places left to settle. Perhaps one year they would manage to overpower the villagers, and take this town for their own.

But whatever the original reason, it did not matter now. The Visitors came here because every year, on the longest day, at midnight, they invaded the river town, and stole what they could, and usually made off with enough to last them until next year.

More than anything, then, they came to the river town because it was what they had always done.

On the night before the longest day, Nathaniel couldn't sleep, his thoughts buzzing with half-formed images of the Visitors.

He remembered them from years past, but this year was different.

This year, he was twelve years old, and Father was dead. This year, it was Nathaniel's turn to prove himself to the Elders, to lead the younger children in their defense of the village and earn the right to be called a man, and with Father gone . . .

Well. With Father gone, everything had changed in all the worst ways. Mother's eyes had turned dull and blank, their house was now silent as a stone's belly, and Gerta, Nathaniel's little sister, was prone to unexpected crying fits that left Nathaniel feeling angry and wrung out, for there was nothing he could do to help her.

But he could do this. He could defend his town from the Visitors.

And he *would*.

On the longest day, he sat on the roof and watched as the adults filed underground, into the caverns. His mother's dress was a flash of familiar blue fabric. He heard the latches of the heavy wooden doors click shut, and the low rumble of the boulders being rolled into place behind them.

Then, silence. A red-feathered eagle cried out, gliding high overhead.

Gerta came out of the house and squinted up at Nathaniel, holding her slingshot. "Don't you want to practice with me?"

"No," he said. "Practice with Edith. I must keep watch."

And he did, all day, watching the black river coil through the prairie grasses until his eyes turned scratchy and dry.

In his fist, he clutched his father's old sword — a relic passed down through the generations, from a nobler age. That's what Father had always said. An age when the Visitors had not yet come to taint the land with their filth.

"So that is why we must fight them?" Nathaniel had asked, once. "Because they are dirty?"

"We fight them because that is what happens, at midnight on the longest day of the year," his father had answered. "We fight them because they are low forms of life, and if they are allowed to enter our lands, they will poison us with their dirty blood, their savage customs." Father had leaned close, placed a heavy hand on each of Nathaniel's shoulders. "They are not welcome here."

"But *why*?" Nathaniel had pressed. There had to be a particular reason. Father was always telling him to examine situations, to take them apart and thoroughly think over each piece.

"Why do vermin invade our cupboards?"

Nathaniel had frowned. "Because they must eat?"

Father, nodding, had then said, "But does that mean we should allow them to chew our belongings, steal our food, spread disease?"

"No, of course not."

And then Nathaniel's eyes had widened, and he had understood.

The Visitors were vermin. They could not help being nasty, low, vile invaders — but they must nevertheless be stopped.

★ ★ ★

At sundown, the oldest children donned their armor — dull metal gauntlets and breastplates, cinched with soft leather straps. They pulled on their helmets, their faces shielded with slatted visors.

The adults, underground, had no armor. They had no need for it. The only day anyone needed armor anymore was on the longest day, and even then, it was the responsibility of the children to defend the town. It was a way of proving oneself to the Elders, earning the right to be part of the community.

Nathaniel had dreamed of this day every night since Father's death. He counted the minutes to midnight by watching the moon's progress in the sky.

Then a shriek rang out, from the far bend of the river.

Nathaniel jumped down from the roof, climbed the town gates, held up his sword. His arm shook beneath its weight, but not as much as it used to.

"Ready yourselves!" he cried, and the children below climbed the watchtowers, pulled their bowstrings, sharpened their daggers one last time, prepared the stones for the catapults. Little Gerta waved happily at Nathaniel with her slingshot hand.

Then, with a hiss of sound, the first Visitor scurried through the gates. Nathaniel almost didn't see it, distracted as he was by Gerta. But the *smell* of a Visitor — sour and rotten — *that* he couldn't possibly miss.

He looked wildly about; saw the hulking shape of a Visitor slinking along the inner wall, in the shadows created by the children's array of torches.

"They're here!" Nathaniel cried. "Attack! *Attack!*"

The children leaped down from their perches, launching themselves into the clumps of Visitors now making their way in from the prairie. Some of the Visitors moved like worms, crawling with their bellies flat to the ground. Others relied solely on speed, running headlong at the food stores kept in the center of town, their cloaks streaming behind them.

Nathaniel shuddered to hear their unearthly cries, but nevertheless jumped down from the town gates, ready to fight. For a moment, he stood there in the road, and simply took in the chaos of it — children chasing Visitors, throwing stones and screaming their fury; Visitors, scrabbling madly at locked doors until they were pulled down and swarmed upon by children grasping wooden clubs.

Nathaniel should have chosen the nearest Visitor and lunged at him with his sword. He had practiced doing so hundreds of times since Father died and the sword became rightfully his.

But . . .

Something about the sounds these Visitors made as they were stoned, as they were beaten and then lay moaning and twitching in the road, seemed familiar to Nathaniel. It took him a moment to pin down the feeling, standing there immobile as the other children ran frenzied around him and the Visitors cried out in pain.

Yes, that was it. *Pain*.

He had heard those pained cries earlier that year, as Father lay dying in his sickbed. As the fever took him, racking his body with seizures. As he fought to draw his last few breaths, so that he could tell Nathaniel how much he loved him, one last time.

Yes, Nathaniel had heard those sounds before, and hearing them now made him wonder — could the Visitors feel pain, just as his people could? The thought slammed into him with the force of a hundred fists.

"Wait," Nathaniel said, though it came out as a mere gust of air. The magnitude of what he was about to do held him there, in that one spot, breathless. Then he gathered himself, clenched his fists. "Wait! Stop!"

He rushed to the nearest child, pulled back the hand that held the stone, and stood confused over the Visitor cowering on the ground.

"What are you doing?" snapped the other child, his eyes flashing through the slats of his face shield. "I almost had him. Only a couple more blows would've done it."

"I'm not sure," Nathaniel said, staring at the Visitor, torn between what he had been taught and what he felt in the deepest, truest corner of his heart. "I just want to wait for a moment. I think . . . I think we should all wait. I think we're hurting them."

"Are you *mad*?" spat the child. "Of course we're hurting them! They've come to take our food. We have to protect our people. Get off of me. What's wrong with you?"

"But my father . . . when he died, he—"

A piercing scream rang out, from deeper in the village. A scream that was as familiar to Nathaniel as the sound of his own voice.

Gerta. Gerta, *afraid*.

Nathaniel forgot everything else and ran toward the scream, followed by the sounds of the child behind him resuming his duties.

Left, right, right, another left, Nathaniel raced into the center of town—and there, not far from their hut, was Gerta.

She crouched on the ground in her armor, cradling her arm. The sick angle of it made Nathaniel's stomach turn. It had to have been broken.

Not far from her, a Visitor hovered uncertainly. Soft clicks and murmurs drifted out from beneath its pale mask.

A surge of rage scorched Nathaniel clean, erasing everything from his mind and heart but the need to protect and hurt.

Protect Gerta. Hurt what had hurt her.

And in this moment of rage, an idea came to him, clear and simple, sharp as the blade he now placed on the ground. He could no longer use the sword; it would be over too quickly.

The thing that had hurt Gerta deserved something . . . slower.

At his movement, the Visitor's head snapped toward him.

"It's all right, I won't hurt you," said Nathaniel, forcing his voice calm. He took off his helmet; a rush of air cooled his face. "I don't want to fight anymore."

The Visitor reared back, as if surprised; it clicked and murmured a question.

Nathaniel held up his hands and slowly moved toward the door of his hut. "Look. I'm not hurting you. I don't want to fight. We have food in here. You can have some, if you want. Don't you want some food?"

The Visitor continued tilting its head in confusion.

"Nathaniel?" came Gerta's tearful whisper.

Nathaniel ignored her. "Come on. Come inside." He felt as though he were coaxing a dog. Father's words returned to him — *Why do vermin invade our cupboards?* — and Nathaniel flushed with shame to remember how close he had come to betraying everyone.

He stepped inside the hut and quickly went to prepare everything in the kitchen, his heart pounding, his hands shaking. Gerta, crying. Gerta, screaming. The vermin. The *filth*.

The Visitor shuffled inside, bringing with it a stench of unwashed skin. Nathaniel's mouth turned bitter with hatred.

"Here," he said, holding a plate and cup, the tips of his fingers still stinging from when he had dipped them into his mother's stash of webcap powder. In small doses, the powder was useful in treating sickness.

In large doses, however, it was fatal.

Nathaniel held out the plate and cup. He hoped the Visitor

couldn't smell the webcap powder lacing the juice and mixed into the hash.

He swallowed hard against the mix of excitement and revulsion in his throat, and smiled.

"Have some," he said cheerfully.

The Visitor hesitated for only a moment, and then grabbed for the plate. It untied its mask, flung it away, removed its gloves, and began scooping sloppy handfuls of hash into its mouth.

A mouth not filled with poisoned fangs, as Nathaniel had been taught.

A mouth that contained flat white teeth like his, bordered by two lips, like his. And hands that were covered with skin, and five-fingered.

Nathaniel stood, paralyzed with first surprise and then horror, as he understood what he was seeing.

"But you're—you're not—" he stuttered.

The Visitor looked up at him, crumbs lining his mouth. "Food?" it said, holding up the plate of hash.

No, not *it*. *Him*.

The Visitor was not a monster, not a vermin.

The Visitor was a boy.

"I don't understand," Nathaniel said, walking backward until he hit the wall. "This can't be right."

For the Visitor didn't look exactly like Nathaniel, no—he had sickly white skin, pale eyes, pale hair. Obviously his kind were not people who typically dwelled in sunlight. But he had a nose like Nathaniel, and ten fingers, and two ears, and though

Nathaniel couldn't understand the language, he had the sickening feeling that the Visitor now babbling excitedly on his kitchen floor was trying to thank him.

This Visitor did not look much older than Nathaniel himself. And when the Visitor looked up to smile, his mouth full of food, Nathaniel thought that the boy even looked . . . *kind*.

"Wait," Nathaniel managed to whisper at last, when the shock began to let go of him. "Wait, stop." He rushed at the Visitor, kicked away the plate and cup. "Stop it! Stop eating!"

But the Visitor had already begun to choke, clutching his own throat with pale, wiry hands. Memories seized Nathaniel—the gagging, despairing sounds of Father's sickbed; how he had writhed in pain. The memories drowned out even the battle cries from outside.

The Visitor's grasping fingers were too long, too thin, but they were familiar enough, similar enough, to bring a word to Nathaniel's mind:

Friend. This Visitor—this *boy*—could have been a *friend*.

The word shot through Nathaniel with the force of an arrow, leaving an empty feeling behind, for it had come to him too late.

Mike Winchell

IF ONLY...

Dealing
with Regret, Guilt,
and Sadness

After my parents had divorced and

I was still living with my mom, my Aunt Margie babysat me once in a while. She and Mom weren't just sisters; they were best friends. As Christmas was approaching that year, Aunt Margie had brought me to a toy store and asked me to pick something I wanted for Christmas. I looked at all the toy vehicles, and told her I wanted this toy army jeep. I remember that Christmas looking and looking for the present from Aunt Margie, and when I found it, all I could think of was the army jeep. But when I opened it, it was this toy van and not the jeep.

I bawled and bawled, so disappointed I hadn't gotten the toy I'd wanted. Aunt Margie called soon after we'd opened presents and she'd heard me crying and complaining that I hadn't gotten the jeep. The thing is, I ended up loving that toy van, but for some reason I couldn't bring myself to tell her that. In the end, the unwanted toy experience left me with feelings I had a hard time dealing with.

When I was in seventh grade Aunt Margie passed away, and the feelings hit me even harder. I had other memories with her, but that toy van dominated my mind when she died. I regretted not telling Aunt Margie I loved the toy van, and I felt guilty about how I'd acted like a spoiled brat when I hadn't gotten the jeep I'd originally wanted. It stung to think about how it must have made her feel to spend money on me, only to have me act ungrateful.

Julia Alvarez, Linda Sue Park, and Lisa Yee know what it's like to feel those same emotions, and they show how it's natural to look back and wonder "if only I had done something differently" when these experiences take place.

Julia Alvarez

MY FIRST TRUE FRENEMY

When I was ten years old, my family escaped the dictatorship of Trujillo in the Dominican Republic. My father had been part of an underground group of freedom fighters, several of whom were arrested. When the dictator's police began patrolling our house and keeping track of every move we made, my father knew that he was next. We managed to get out with the help of a contact in the CIA who forged a letter, inviting my father to come to the United States to study heart surgery.

The dictatorship didn't allow many people to leave, so we were lucky to get our passports. Or so my parents kept telling my sisters and me once we landed in New York City. But I didn't feel lucky at all. I was terribly homesick for my cousins and my family. It was hard to make friends, because I didn't know English very well, and besides, my parents had gotten even stricter here. They were relieved to be in this country but also afraid of it. They didn't know the rules. One wrong move and we might be deported.

You'd think I'd be happy once school started. A chance to make friends. A chance to get out of that tiny, confining apartment. But I was afraid, too. What if I didn't understand the teacher? Back then, immigrant children were not encouraged to be bilingual. What if I forgot and spoke Spanish to one of my sisters in the playground? Would we all be sent back home, where my father, and maybe our whole family, would be killed?

The first day of school, I walked into a classroom full of American kids, who all seemed bigger, blonder, fairer. And smarter. (They knew perfect English, after all!) But then, I spotted a girl who looked like one of my cousins. She turned out to be Dominican, too. But unlike me, she knew a lot of English because she had been in the States for a while. Her father was some sort of diplomat. I didn't know much about what diplomats did; all I knew was that finally I had a friend to help me navigate my way in this new school and language.

But when I got home full of my good news, my parents were not happy at all. It turned out that this girl's father was a big supporter of the dictator, and that's why he had been appointed to represent our country. One wrong word from me, and the girl might tell her parents, who might communicate this information to authorities back home. My uncles and their families would be wiped out. And even my own, immediate family could be in danger. A few years before our arrival, Galíndez, a Dominican exile who had criticized the dictator, had been kidnapped from New York City, taken back, tortured, and killed.

Every day before I left for school, my mother would go

through her list of reminders of what I had to be careful not to say to this girl.

I tried to keep my distance. But she was so nice to me. She helped me with my homework. She explained things I didn't understand in English. She brought me treats her maid cooked—yes, her family had a staff. Meanwhile, I had to invent stories about why I couldn't accept her invitations or reciprocate with gifts. I had to pretend that my parents were big supporters of the dictator.

Late one night, we got a call in our apartment. The dictator had been assassinated by a rebel group, which included some of my uncles. My parents were elated. Our country would soon be free. We would be able to go back.

My friend was not at school the following morning. In fact, I don't remember much about her after that day. In my memory, she just fades away—except for our last conversation. She told me that her parents had been crying ever since they got the horrible news. It was as if a family member had died. I couldn't tell her that there was great rejoicing in my family. I didn't want to hurt her feelings. Also, for so many months I had been telling her stories about how my family also liked the dictator. I didn't know how to get over the tall barrier of lies I had been forced by circumstances to tell.

THROUGH THE CHAIN-LINK FENCE

Through the chain-link fence, Taty could see her new school, a big stone building with bars on the bottom windows. Her heart pounded. She wondered if her mother could hear it above the noise of traffic on the busy city street.

"It looks like a prison," Taty whined. They had just escaped a dictatorship, full of people in jail. Wasn't this country supposed to be better?

Her mother sighed. She was sick and tired of Taty's complaints. "I already explained, it's to keep burglars out."

"But what would a burglar want to steal from a school?" Taty persisted. Her mother was silent. "Mami? Will there be anybody I know?" In the Dominican Republic, her whole school had been full of cousins.

Her mother sighed again. "I don't know." Before they arrived in this country, Mami had known everything. But here, in New York City, it seemed those three words were her mother's constant reply to every question Taty asked. *Yo no sé.*

"What if I don't understand the English?" Taty asked her mother in Spanish.

Her mother leveled *that* look at her. Taty didn't have to know any language to understand what it meant: *Not one more word from you!* They had fled to the United States to be free, but her mother had gotten even stricter here. Taty felt like Mami was having no problem picking up where the dictator had left off.

Their last month on the island, police started patrolling their house and following Mami and Papi whenever they went out. Her father was in some kind of trouble with the dictator. "Why are the police after us?" Taty kept asking. Her mother would turn *that* look on her. This wasn't a case of her mother not knowing—Mami knew—but she was not about to tell Taty.

From her cousins, Taty learned that her uncle and her father were in some kind of secret "underground" to get rid of the dictator and bring freedom to the country. When Taty had asked her mother if it was true, Mami had gone berserk—yanking her by the arm, hurrying her down the hallway, locking the bedroom door, and then yanking her again, this time into the walk-in closet, where Taty had recently discovered some hidden guns she was punished for discovering. "You are going to get your father and all of us killed, unless you keep quiet!" her mother whispered fiercely.

"Quiet about what?"

"About what your parents say or do at home, about what your uncles and aunts say in their houses . . ." Her mother's list went on and on. How was Taty supposed to remember so many things? She might as well not talk at all.

★ ★ ★

Soon after their arrival in New York City, her father had taken her to see the Statue of Liberty. "Pray that good luck comes to everybody back home," he told Taty, touching the stone of the statue as if it were the Virgin in the cathedral. Now that they were free, Papi had explained a bit more about the dictatorship. People who were suspected of being against the dictator were being incarcerated, tortured, killed. Her uncles were in danger. But soon . . . soon . . . soon . . . Her father never seemed to be able to finish that sentence.

Soon, school started, but the situation back home wasn't any better. Taty didn't care. She wanted to go back. Every night when her family said prayers, she'd burst into tears. She was so lonely. She missed her cousins terribly, and her uncles and aunts, and her dog, Luna, and the ponies on her grandfather's *finca*, and the taste of mangoes and guavas and coconut water, and the endless beaches with teensy crabs scuttling across the warm sand . . .

Taty's list was even longer than the list of things she hadn't been able to talk about back on the island.

As Taty entered her class, her heart was a moth caught in a lamp shade trying to get free. She looked around at the boys and girls, none of them familiar, many with light coloring, most of them taller, older, and smarter-looking than she. They had to be smarter: they knew how to speak English!

Her teacher, a plump, kindly-looking nun, introduced herself: Sister Something. Even though Taty had learned classroom English back home, she couldn't make out what her teacher was saying. Americans spoke so quickly, their words all running together.

"Somethingsomethingsomething." Sister Something bent down so she was eye level with Taty. Her eyes were little bits of blue sky, which made her look even more religious than the dark habit and headdress she was wearing.

She led Taty toward a desk by the window. And that's when Taty spotted her. A girl her size, with her coloring, same dark, curly hair.

"Lucy, this is Taty Castillo. She's Dominican, too." The nun smiled beneficently, as Lucy greeted Taty with a burst of English. Even so, Taty could guess what Lucy was saying, because like most Dominicans, her face was so expressive.

The minute the nun turned away, Lucy whispered, *"Hablo Español."* They could speak in Spanish, but they had to be careful, so as not to get caught. It was almost as if they were back home in the underground!

During recess, the two girls chatted away in Spanish, falling silent only when Sister Zoey (that was their teacher's name, Lucy told Taty) or some other teacher approached them.

Lucy was actually Lucía Ramos. She knew "Taty" was the Dominican nickname for Altagracia, a name you could never use in this country. "Imagine! You'd have to be spelling it all the time. Hey, we could just say you're High Grace Castle, and I'm

Lucy Branches, get it? I guess not," she answered herself after a beat. "Once you know English, you can tell a lot of jokes that most people won't get."

Taty felt like one of those people now, so she changed the subject. "How long have you been here?"

"Almost two years. And before that Washington, DC, so that's how come I speak a lot of English. My father's the Dominican consul," Lucía went on to explain. Before Taty could ask what a consul was, Lucía asked her, "Where does your father work?"

Taty wasn't ready to confess to Lucía that her father couldn't work as a doctor in this country. He had to pass a license exam, but first he had to learn English. He was taking a night class after working all day as a janitor in a hospital. They were living in a tiny apartment about the size of their living room back home. "At some hospital," Taty answered vaguely.

At the end of the day, as Taty and her new friend descended the front steps, a sleek black car pulled up in front of the school. The uniformed driver came around and opened the back door. A woman in dark glasses leaned out. Lucía introduced her mother.

"Una dominicana? Excelente!" The mother seemed pleased that Taty was Dominican. She launched into a whole bunch of questions about Taty's family. What was her father's surname? Her mother's? Were they related to this or that other family with the same last names?

This was so typical. Every time Dominicans met, they

started figuring out where they all belonged in the country's forest of family trees. It seemed everyone was related to everyone else.

"Shall we give you a ride home?"

But Taty could already see her mother coming down the street, waving.

★ ★ ★

"I made a friend, Mami!" Those were the first words in Spanish out of Taty's mouth. Her mother smiled with relief. Taty knew Mami worried a lot about Taty's homesickness. "And guess what? Guess what?"

Her mother could not guess.

So Taty told her all about Lucía, a Dominican girl in her class, who knew a lot of English, whose family had lived in Washington, DC. "They must be rich, Mami. They have a big fancy car with a chauffeur . . . What's wrong?"

Instead of that joyous look of a minute ago, Mami's face was washed of color. She asked Taty the first question Mrs. Ramos had just asked her: What was Lucía's last name?

"Ramos."

Mami stopped and turned to Taty. "What did you tell her? Tell me what you told her!" Mami had grabbed Taty's shoulders and was shaking her. As if they were back on the island. As if they hadn't gotten free, after all.

That night, when Papi got back from English class, there was a family conference in the small bedroom where they all slept. Papi explained that Señor Ramos was the Dominican consul, which meant he represented the dictator. "We left all the family there. We would not want them to be in danger. And the dictator has a long arm," Papi added. "Enemies of the regime have disappeared from here, too."

"But this girl is my friend," Taty pleaded.

Her father nodded sadly. "She is probably a very nice girl. But the dictator is an evil man. It's fine to be friends with this girl. But you have to be careful what you say. You have to keep your distance. You can't trust her with anything private."

So what was the point of having a friend if you couldn't do any of the things friends did with each other?

Then Mami went through her whole list again, adding even more things Taty must remember not to say. The Mami Dictatorship was never, ever going to go away!

★ ★ ★

It was so confusing: being someone's friend, but your parents were her enemies — secret enemies at that.

At every turn, Lucía asked questions about things on Mami's Remember-Not-to-Talk-about-It list. At first, Taty was suspicious. Maybe her friend was spying on the Castillos for her father. But the whole Ramos family seemed genuinely friendly, inviting Taty's parents to functions, sending them a Christmas card.

Meanwhile, Taty had to keep inventing stories. Then she had to remember what she had invented so that Lucía wouldn't suspect her of lying.

Taty's father had come to the US to learn to do heart

transplants so he could save lives back home. Her family supported the dictator. The reason she couldn't go over to Lucía's house was because . . . because she had to help her mother clean the apartment, wash the dishes, iron their clothes.

"Don't you have a maid?" Lucía wanted to know.

Um . . . Um . . . The maid had quit and taken a job cleaning in a hospital.

"You poor thing!" Lucía threw her arms around her. Taty felt like a creep. She wondered: Was it a sin to lie as much as she did? And to a friend? But she couldn't ask the priest at confession because then she'd be talking about things on Mami's list, which would be breaking the commandment about obeying your parents, which was definitely a sin.

★ ★ ★

Late one night, the phone rang in the apartment. "They did it! They did it!" Papi cried out. Taty's uncles had killed the dictator! Mami was on her knees; Papi knelt beside her. They were praying, laughing, hugging each other.

It was good when evil people died, but should good people be so happy about killing someone bad? The older Taty got, the more confusing life was becoming! Like having two languages: You had a lot more choices, but also a lot more chances to make mistakes, say the wrong thing, get people killed, and sometimes even kill them yourself.

★ ★ ★

The next morning, Lucía was not at school, but Taty was not surprised. Probably, the Ramos family had not gotten much sleep, either. But days went by, and Lucía did not return to class. Meanwhile, it was all over the news: the dictator had been deposed. Taty's uncles were now heroes.

A week later, during recess, the black car pulled up to the curb. The chauffeur came around. First Lucía, then her mother climbed out.

"Lucía!" Taty was so relieved to see her friend.

Lucía exchanged a few words with her mother. Then, as Mrs. Ramos climbed the steps into the building, Lucía walked over to the chain-link fence. Her eyes were red, her face puffy. She peered at Taty through the links with the same look as Mami's when she was upset with Taty.

"Your family killed our *jefe*! You lied to me. All these months you pretended you were our friends."

"I am your friend!" Taty had told Lucía many lies to protect her family, but this was the truth.

"We have to leave. We can't stay here. Papi's already getting death threats! Mami came to get my stuff." Now Lucía was sobbing so hard, Taty thought her own heart would break. She wanted to reach out and comfort Lucía. To assure her they were friends, even if their parents were enemies. But Taty couldn't come up with the words to express her feelings. She was forgetting her Spanish, and her English had not yet caught up with everything in her heart.

Mrs. Ramos was already heading down the steps, carrying a stuffed shopping bag, Sister Zoey by her side. "Lucía," she called.

"Okay, Mami." Lucía turned back to Taty. She had stopped crying, but her face was flushed. Her eyes were two windows about to be clamped shut against an oncoming storm. But before they closed on her forever, Taty caught a glimpse of her friend thinking of the worst thing she could say to wound her new enemy.

"Te odio!" Lucía spit the words out in Spanish, and then, as if to make them doubly strong, she repeated them in English: "I hate you!" She clenched her fingers around the links as if they were Taty's eyes she wanted to scratch out. Taty drew back, feeling the force of that emotion. No one had ever said they hated her in her whole life.

Later, Taty would think of all the things she could have said, a whole list of explanations, apologies, or on angry days, words more hurtful back. She wanted a different ending to their story instead of what she remembered: Lucía climbing into the car, never looking back, as Taty watched from the other side of a fence that had always been there between the two friends.

THE VOICE

n seventh-grade English class at O. W. Huth Junior High School, Mrs. Gregerson called on Barry to read aloud.

Barry had red hair and glasses and very pale skin and sat three seats behind me. Like a lot of other boys that year, his voice was changing. But nobody else's was changing as dramatically as Barry's was.

I sat in my seat, listening to him read. In the middle of page forty-two of *The Pearl*, Barry's voice cracked and broke and skidded with a startling high-pitched squeak that made the whole class laugh, including Mrs. Gregerson.

And Barry laughed, too. I turned around to see that even though those pale cheeks of his were turning raspberry red, he was laughing right along with the rest of us.

From then on, whenever Mrs. Gregerson wanted something read aloud, she almost always asked Barry. All year long, through *The Pearl* and *A Separate Peace* and *Lord of the Flies*, we knew that a couple times a week, we'd get to have a really good laugh in class.

★ ★ ★

The end-of-year tradition for seventh-graders at O. W. Huth was a trip to the state capital. I could hardly wait. Janet and Dawn and I talked about it for weeks, planning what to bring and discussing—gleefully—what it would be like to spend a weekend in a nice hotel with only a few helpless chaperones trying to control the whole seventh grade.

It took forever to get there, but at least we got to ride on real coaches, not school buses. The hotel was very cool—a fancy lobby, balconies, a game room.

And a big indoor pool.

On the first day, we toured some of the Important Sights in the capital. At least, that was what we were supposed to be doing. Mostly we whispered and giggled and stood near, but not *too* near, the boys we thought were cute. The tour wasn't the fun part. All of us knew the *real* fun would happen later that evening: the pool pizza party.

Back at the hotel, we changed into our bathing suits and spent ages trying to decide how to wrap our towels around our waists. Then we took the elevator down to the lobby. I caught a glimpse of Barry in his swim trunks. His bare chest was unbelievably pale; I figured that only an albino could possibly be whiter.

The pool was so crowded that I could hardly see any of the blue of the water. It was packed with kids waving their arms, screaming at their friends, bobbing up and down because there certainly wasn't room to swim.

The noise was incredible. The sound of hundreds of yelling

kids seemed to be multiplied exponentially by the tiled walls. Janet and Dawn and I didn't even have to say anything to one another: We left the pool area without a backward glance.

Outside on the patio, we got our pizza. As we were eating, kids began streaming out of the pool—everyone all at once, it seemed. It was complete chaos, kids milling around, chaperones yelling, hotel employees dashing about in panic.

It was a few hours before we found out what had happened.

Barry had drowned in the pool. I had never known anyone my age who had died before, and at first I couldn't believe it. Our trip was cut short; we got back on the coaches to go home that night. Throughout the whole ride, I kept replaying the evening in my mind.

I was almost positive that I had seen Barry out on the patio while we were eating pizza. So there must have been some mistake.

I was wrong.

There was no mistake. Barry was dead, and I would never again hear his voice behind me in English class.

But I would hear it in my head at odd moments. In the locker corridor at school. In bed when I was half asleep. Other places, other times, always when I wasn't expecting it.

Even now, more than forty years later, I sometimes still hear it.

THE STORY

THE HONORABLE MENTION

mmaculate white pants with knife-edge creases.

Crisp navy blue shirt, bright red tie.

His red hair shining, combed, perfect.

Glasses framing his eyes, making him look so distinguished.

He looked awesome—from a distance. Closer up, though, I noticed a couple things that really weirded me out.

★ ★ ★

We'd won the regional, so the O. W. Smith Junior High School chorus was getting ready for State. The All-State Select Chorus competition. Thirty of us—eighteen girls, twelve boys—would be heading down to Springfield, our state capital, to sing against a bunch of other schools. The chorus qualifying for State was practically the biggest thing that had ever happened at Smith.

Three songs. We practiced them a million times each. My favorite was the one from *Grease*.

Girls: *We go together*

Boys: *Like rama-lama-lama, kadingy kading-a-dong*

Girls: *Remember forever*

Boys: *As shoo-bop, shoo-wadda wadda, yippity boom-de-boom*

I could hear Larry Harris singing his part (tenor), and I tried to sing mine (alto) just as well, maybe even a little better. Which wasn't easy, because Larry Harris had a voice like an angel.

Okay, I didn't know that for a fact because I'd never heard an angel sing, and even people who have, like in the Bible, don't do a very good job describing it. They don't say if all angels sing soprano, or what kind of music they sing, or if there are solo parts, and it's always a "heavenly host," so any harpists would get drowned out for sure.

But if I ever *did* hear an angel sing, I thought they'd make the kind of music that you could listen to for hours and hours, forever and ever, and never get tired of, so when it stops you'd feel like crying out loud, "No! Keep going! Please!" and that was what it felt like when I heard Larry sing.

In chorus, Larry stood just behind me and a little to my right, so I got to have his awesome voice in my right ear. I told my best friend, Janice, that being able to hear him so easily made me sing better, and right away she asked, "Do you like him?"

I said, "No, I like his voice, that's all."

Janice is my best friend, my soul mate, my twin, but it seems like every time I mention a boy's name, she wants to know if I like him, and sometimes that gets boring.

Even though he had a great voice, Larry never tried out for a solo. Other people said it was because he was kind of—well, *odd* looking. Red hair. Freckles. Glasses, the kind with thick black rims.

But I knew the real reason, even though we'd never talked about it. I could feel it when we were singing.

Larry tried to blend his voice with everyone else's, and I tried to do the same. I loved the sound of a whole bunch of people singing together, how all those mouths and voices singing all those different notes could merge together like silk, with no single voice sticking out.

It was a much bigger feeling than someone singing alone, no matter how good they were. The kids who were obsessed with getting solo parts didn't understand that. People were always telling me that I should try for a solo, too, but I thought singing in a group was much more fun. Especially if you were standing really close to Angel-Voice Boy.

In Select Chorus, it didn't matter if you were fat and black (like Sandra), or fat and white (like Beth), or had bad skin (like Corey), or needed special help in reading (like Jason), or were custodied jointly (like a lot of kids), or got free lunch (we weren't supposed to know who, but we did — Ashton, Kendall, Hannah), or were short and flat-chested and unathletic and Asian and liked reading more than hanging out most of the time (like me).

Only two things mattered:

You could sing, and you loved to sing.

★ ★ ★

Still. It wasn't always easy to get thirty people to sing the right notes at the right time with the right kind of feeling. Mr. Scott, our chorus teacher, said it was like trying to put a straitjacket on an octopus. You got four of the arms tied up neatly, but then the fifth clamped its suckers on a rock and couldn't be budged, while six, seven, and eight jerked around wildly doing any old thing.

We weren't *wahoo*ing right. We were supposed to hold the *-hoo* for two counts and then cut it off quickly with a *YEAH!* as close to a shout as we could get while still singing.

Wa-hoooooooo YEAH!

Mr. Scott kept his hands open during the *-hoo,* then snapped them shut into fists on the *yeah,* like he was trying to grab the octopus. But it was no use, no matter how many times we tried it. Sometimes the sopranos were fine but the altos messed up; the next time the tenors and mezzos were good but the sopranos were off, and the poor basses, they were that fifth arm clamped ferociously on the wrong beat every time.

Finally, Mr. Scott stopped conducting and turned away from us, rubbing his head like he was in an aspirin commercial, and Mrs. Rizzo stopped playing the piano, so the quiet was very loud.

Mr. Scott paced in front of us for a while, then stopped, took a deep breath, and said, "Everyone close your eyes."

Some kids started to giggle, but we all closed our eyes, at least I think everyone did but I couldn't see, and then he said, "Picture a big sharp knife. A meat cleaver. It comes down hard, like a karate chop, wham! Right when my hands close. Can you see it?"

He continued. "That knife is the *YEAH!* and it's cutting off the *-hoo*, got it? Everybody see it? Okay, let's go."

We opened our eyes to see him nod at Mrs. Rizzo. The piano gave us a four-bar lead, and here we go again . . .

Wa-hooooooooo—

and this time we all chopped down hard *right* when his hands closed, and every last one of us was dead on—

YEAH!

The bus trip to Springfield was like a miniature version of the cafeteria, on wheels. The popular kids sat in one clot, with Suzanne bossing everyone around; the black kids in another clot, with Sandra as their queen; the rest of us scattered around in twos and threes.

Janice and I were a tiny clot in our wide cushy seats that reclined (a little, anyway), a giant window to the left, a TV for videos overhead. We had potato chips and power drinks. Books and CDs. Chocolate. And most important of all for a trip like this—*pillows*.

The first couple hours were noisy, kids shouting and throwing stuff across the aisles, but then we settled down to read or listen to music or look out the window at mile after mile after mile of greenness, so vast and flat and never-endingly numbing that after a while I started to feel almost proud of it. Who needed scenic old mountains when you could look at a gazillion fields of high-yield corn?

As we got closer to Springfield, good old Abe Lincoln started turning up everywhere. The Lincoln Diner, Honest Abe's

Hardware, Lincoln Funeral Home. Even Lincoln Doughnuts. For us, though, there was only one real Lincoln: the Lincoln Hotel.

We staggered off the bus after seven hours, but it was worth it because the hotel was *so* cool. The lobby had a gigantic chandelier, the biggest one I'd ever seen. All our rooms had cute little balconies. There was a decent game room, good vending machines, and—YESSS!!!—a big indoor pool. Which we immediately dubbed the Emancipation Pool.

It was partly the chaperones' fault that the first night was so crazy, because their lights-out time was totally ridiculous. Did they really think we'd go to sleep at *nine* o'clock?

I was sharing a room with Janice, Hannah, and Beth. We were bouncing from bed to bed, phoning all the other rooms, tossing stuff back and forth to other kids on the balconies. The parent chaperones kept walking up and down the halls and yelling. We'd get into bed and pretend to settle down when they checked our room, but we were up again as soon as they were gone.

It was crazy fun, but I started to get a little tired. I wanted to read and then go to sleep. Didn't anyone else care about the competition in the morning? I stomped into the bathroom and locked myself in.

Janice pounded on the door and convinced me to open up. We sat, her on the edge of the bathtub, me on the closed lid of the toilet.

"We're going to be terrible tomorrow if we don't get some sleep," I said.

She reached over and patted my shoulder. "We'll be okay. I mean, we've practiced enough, don't you think? Twice a day, before school and after, for the past three weeks."

"Yeah," I said, "but you sing better when you're not tired."

I guess Janice saw that it wasn't going to be easy to cheer me up, so she took the detachable shower head off the bathtub wall and held it like a microphone. I knew what she had in mind, and my bad mood started to slide away.

"We go together," she sang, and then stuck the shower head in front of my face.

"Like rama-lama-lama, kadingy-kading-a-dong."

I couldn't help smiling. Singing always made me feel better.

Why do bathrooms have such great acoustics? I put one hand on my ear, miming like I was using headphones in a recording studio. Janice laughed.

We kept singing, and halfway through, I realized that the other girls must have heard us, because they were singing, too.

Janice opened the bathroom door, and the balcony doors were already open, so by the time we started the song again, the girls up and down our hall, and the boys one floor above us, had all joined in, everyone clustered on their balconies singing *shoo-bop, shoo wadda-wadda yippity boom-de-boom . . .*

I listened for Larry's voice, but I couldn't pick it out—he was blending it with everyone else's.

The song was really upbeat, but it faded out at the end with lots of repeats:

We'll always / be together . . . We'll always / be together . . .

As we sang the ending over and over, people started sort of fading out themselves, in ones and twos, until at last it was quiet, and we all went to bed.

"See," Janice whispered sleepily into my ear, "I told you we'd be okay."

And we were.

Better than okay.

When we sang in front of the judges, our *wahoo-yeah* was perfect, and Mr. Scott looked so happy, it almost made me laugh.

Larry sang even better than usual, his notes clear and pure, and for all three songs I tried to match him. We sounded so good together, I felt like we took the whole chorus with us. And then . . .

Honorable Mention.

Which was the same as fourth place.

We'd beaten out much bigger choruses from schools that had made the finals for years.

We were jumping up and down, screaming, high-fiving each other so much that my hand got sore. I could hardly wait to get home and tell my family and everyone at school all about it. And when Mr. Donaldson, the principal, got the news by phone, he said to have a pizza party that night, his treat.

The pizza party was going to be held at the pool. Janice and I changed into our swimsuits. On our way down to the pool, we checked out everyone else—casually, of course—and discussed which guys were the hottest.

I caught a glimpse of Larry and smiled to myself because I couldn't remember ever seeing anyone less tan. His chest and arms and legs were *so* white, and then that red hair—it was like he was another species.

But I didn't say anything to Janice. She'd have asked if I liked him. Again.

The water was *swarming* with kids. It wasn't just our chorus staying at that hotel; a bunch of other schools were there, too. The noise was truly insane—I could see Janice's lips moving, but I couldn't hear what she was saying. The whole place was steamy and reeked of chlorine.

We got our pizza and headed outside through the doors in the big glass wall, to a patio with tables and chairs. We sat on our towels on the grass. It was a lot more peaceful out here. Smelled better, too.

We ate, and talked about the competition, and joked with some of the other kids who came by, especially about the skinny judge, who had sat third from the left, and whose eyebrows were so big and hairy they looked like mice nibbling on his forehead.

I was chewing on my last bite of crust when the glass doors opened and kids started to pour out from the pool area.

More people kept pressing out of the doors behind them. I jumped to my feet and hurried over to the crowd with Janice following me.

"What's going on?" someone asked.

"What happened?" I added.

Everyone around us was dripping wet and shivering and talking at once.

A guy with a megaphone—emergency announcement. "Everyone out of the pool!"

Couldn't even get my towel.

"Go to the nearest exit!"

Couldn't see anything but I heard a girl screaming.

I turned and looked at the glass wall. Kids were lined up along its whole length, their faces pressed against the glass. But it was completely fogged, and we couldn't see a thing.

Then the man with the megaphone came out.

"All students please return to your rooms," he blared. I didn't know who he was, maybe a hotel employee, or someone from another school. "Do not go through the pool area. Go around to the front of the hotel. This is an emergency. Go to your rooms and stay there until further notice."

Everyone started moving toward the front of the hotel.

My stomach was cold. Like I'd just eaten a mozzarella-covered lump of stone.

★ ★ ★

Rumors flew around, crashing into each other madly.

"Maybe somebody got kidnapped."

"Maybe there's a serial killer on the loose."

"Maybe there was too much chlorine in the pool. My cousin got chlorine poisoning once."

By the time we got to the elevators, a few kids were already joking about it.

"Probably nothing," I heard Jason say. "Just a kid getting sick from too much pizza, and a chaperone freaking out about it."

I didn't know what to think.

We waited for ages for our turn on the elevator, and when we got to our room, Hannah and Beth were already there. We called practically everyone else's room, but still couldn't figure out what was happening.

★ ★ ★

A knock on the door.

It was Mrs. Coffey, one of the chaperones. She asked us to go down to her room at the end of the hall. All eighteen of us girls crowded into her room, and Mrs. Coffey closed the door.

"Girls, I'm sorry to have to tell you this. There's been an accident. Apparently Larry Harris dove off the diving board and hit his head on the bottom of the pool."

Gasps.

My heart slowed down—no, not just my heart. Everything. My thoughts came in slow motion.

They must have taken him to the hospital. No, wait— they would have done CPR at the pool first. The lifeguard would know CPR, right? And after that they took him to the hospital . . .

Mrs. Coffey stood next to Hannah. She put her hand on Hannah's shoulder. "Girls, I'm so sorry. No one noticed what happened—there were too many kids, too much noise. By the time they got him up—by the time someone noticed—it was too late. He was already gone."

Gone?

No way.

I *just* saw him. On our way to the pool. And after that . . . while we were eating pizza . . . or in the lobby . . . waiting for the elevators . . . didn't I see him again? Wasn't he there, in the crowd somewhere?

Some girls started crying. That annoyed me for some reason, and I was also annoyed at my stomach, which was still hurting.

"We're cutting our trip short," Mrs. Coffey said. "As you know, we were supposed to tour Springfield tomorrow, but plans have changed. The bus will be leaving in an hour, and we're going to drive all night to get you home. Please go back to your rooms and pack up and be in the lobby before eight o'clock."

★ ★ ★

The ride home was almost completely silent. Most of the kids slept. Janice and I leaned on each other, but didn't talk.

I stared at the seat in front of me, hate hate hating myself because I'd never told Larry how much I liked his voice. Why hadn't I? There were a million times I could have said something—just a few words—*you have a great voice*—that was all I'd have had to say, and I didn't, and now I'd never have another chance.

The bus pulled into the school parking lot in the dead of night, and everybody's parents were there, and everyone was getting hugged, and hugging back, even the boys.

Mr. Donaldson was there, too, and he asked us all to gather

around. We stood in a circle. My mom held my hand, and my dad put his arm around my shoulders. Mr. Donaldson said he was proud of us for the way we behaved during this tragedy. He asked for a moment of silence, and we all bowed our heads.

My tears were hot in my eyes, warm on my cheeks, cold when they got to my chin. My nose started to run, and I didn't know whether to wipe it, or to stand still respectfully.

Then someone started to sing.

"Amazing Grace."

It was Sandra. She sang the first line by herself, then people started joining in, a few at a time. It's almost impossible to cry and sing at the same time, so I had to stop crying. We sounded a little shaky at first, but we finished together strong, the song filling up the chilly darkness.

★ ★ ★

We had school the next day, which seemed so weird, like the world should have changed in some huge way. But it hadn't.

The kids in chorus got a lot of attention—everyone wanted to know where we were, what we saw, and I was proud that none of us said we saw it happen, because we hadn't, and some things are too big to lie about.

A couple days later, the school held a memorial assembly for Larry. Mr. Donaldson walked up to the mic with two other people, and we all knew right away who they were.

Mr. Donaldson told us that Mr. Harris wanted to say a few words. Mr. Harris stepped forward, big and beefy, red hair like

Larry's. Mrs. Harris stood next to him, her head down.

"My wife and I want to thank you all for being friends with Larry," Mr. Harris said. "He loved this school, and he especially loved singing in the chorus. We're glad he was with his friends when — when — "

He stopped, took off his glasses, rubbed his eyes. Put the glasses back on again.

I wondered what happened to Larry's glasses.

Mr. Harris cleared his throat and went on. "We're proud he was with you at State, proud that he was part of — of that Honorable Mention."

He tried to say something more, but finally shook his head and stepped back. Mrs. Harris looked up for just a moment, and I had to put my hand to my mouth to stop from crying out when I saw her face, all hollows and shadows.

The Select Chorus sang "For the Beauty of the Earth," another one of our competition songs. Chorus was officially finished for the year, so we hadn't sung together since our trip. We probably sounded fine to everyone else.

But there was a voice missing in my right ear, and behind my right shoulder, an empty, boy-shaped space.

★ ★ ★

I'd never known anyone my age who'd died before. I imagined Larry doing a nice dive — it would have been a good one, for him to go so deep and hit so hard — and that he never felt a thing, no pain, nothing.

But would he rather have known that he was going to die?

I didn't want to think of him being scared, or hurting, but maybe it could have been like a dream, so he could have thought about his family, or said a little prayer.

★ ★ ★

I heard some of the kids talking about how they were really tight with Larry, great friends, best buds, when I knew they barely knew him.

I hated that because I couldn't decide if he was *my* friend. I didn't want to act like he was if it wasn't true. Was he a friend? Or just a guy I knew? Or maybe even someone I'd started to like a tiny bit?

Larry had ridden the same bus as me. His locker was down the hall from mine. But we'd never hung out together. It was like he'd been in my peripheral vision a lot of the time, but hardly ever in my direct line of sight.

Except in chorus, of course, where I couldn't see him at all unless I turned around.

I remembered his beautiful voice helping me sing better.

I remembered how weird he looked in his swimsuit, but almost cute at the same time.

If you had memories of someone, good memories, did that make them a friend?

Sometimes I felt so bad I thought it meant he was definitely my friend. But was I a fake for feeling that way?

Because hours could go by when I didn't think about him at all.

★ ★ ★

For the funeral, they dressed him in his chorus uniform. White pants, navy blue shirt, red tie. He was wearing his glasses; I was glad, because I'd never seen him without them. He looked dignified, not goofy.

When we went forward to pay our respects, it was weird, the little things I noticed. Makeup was *caked* on his face — so thick it looked like mud, except it was this totally fake pinky-beige color. It was really awful — did they have to do that?

Then I saw his hands, folded over his chest. His nails were manicured. So creepy — they didn't look like a boy's hands.

I sat down again, shaky in my stomach and my knees. Music was playing softly — not funeral music, but a recording of us at State. I sang along inside my head — *rama-lama-lama, kad-ingy-kading-a-dong* — and started to feel a little calmer. Maybe it was impossible to cry and sing at the same time, even if you were only singing inside your head.

I listened hard, but I couldn't pick out Larry's voice.

He'd have liked that.

Lisa Yee

AWKWARD

I n the hilly suburbs that bordered Los Angeles where I grew up, every fourth house looked the same. The floor plans were identical, and if you got out of bed in the middle of the night, and kept your eyes shut, you could find the bathroom (around the corner, down the hall on the left), whether you were at the Liangs', the Kaufmans', or my house.

Most of us moved in at the same time, when the homes were new and the prices were low. But for a kid, the best thing wasn't the shiny new avocado-colored appliances, or the two-car garage, or the view of the city. It was that in most every house on our street there was someone you could play with.

I can recall my family meeting our neighbors for the first time—the adults with overeager smiles, hoping to impress, standing in driveways while their children hid behind them, sizing up the other kids. When I was little, a friend meant someone who would run around in circles with you, and who wouldn't judge you if you dropped your candy bar in the dirt and then ate it. A friend was someone you could explore the woods with, or a person who had a swimming pool—something my family did not own. Later, we were much more discriminating about who we called a friend.

Flash-forward seven years. Some of the friends that I had made when I was five years old stuck, while others fell by the wayside. By the time I hit middle school, cliques had been formed. We shared secrets, talked about boys, and gossiped about other girls.

I'm not sure whose idea it was, but the execution went something like this: I was to hide in the closet, and when Deb came over, June would ask her what she thought of me. "It will be fun," June said.

I wasn't so sure. But I did it anyway. No one ever said no to June.

So I hid in the bedroom closet. It was dark and cramped, and it took my eyes a while to adjust. But when they did, it was fun. June was right. There I was, alone and given permission to eavesdrop. The slats in the closet door let in enough light so I could see some of June's clothes. Unlike me, whose clothes were strewn around the room, hers were hung up neatly on hangers.

"Let's go in my room," I heard June say.

"Is that new?" Deb asked.

As they started to talk about the poster of David Cassidy, a popular heartthrob whose hair was more beautiful than any girl's, June deftly steered the conversation to me. All at once I noticed that there wasn't much air in the closet.

It was suffocating.

"So, what do you think about Lisa?" she said, casually.

"What do you mean?" Deb asked.

June rephrased her question.

"She's nice," Deb volunteered.

Thank you, Deb.

"But is there anything about her that bothers you?" June went on.

There was silence. I held my breath. This was supposed to be fun, but it wasn't.

"No," Deb said, hesitating. "She's nice."

"But isn't there anything about her that bugs you?" June pressed. "Something you can't stand about her?"

I didn't wait for the answer. I didn't want to know. When I burst out of the closet, Deb looked stricken and froze.

June grinned. "She was there the whole time!" she announced proudly.

Deb and I stood there in awkward silence.

I looked at June, who didn't seem to notice that no one else was laughing. That's when it hit me. I may not have known who my friends were, but I now knew who my enemy was.

FUN WITH FRIENDS

O n May 16, Lydia Chan visited Zoe Kaling, uninvited. *Somehow Lydia ended up in the closet of Zoe's room. When Suki Weinstein showed up, Lydia remained in the closet. What she and Zoe had planned was supposed to be fun.*

ZOE KALING

It's not like I even wanted her to come over. She was my next-door neighbor and I had a pool. Lydia was always dropping by and saying things like, "Boy, the water looks inviting."

Then she'd hint and hint until I said, "Do you want to go swimming?"

One time I told Lydia "The pool is closed," but later I got in trouble. My mother claimed I wasn't being neighborly. So the next time Lydia came over, Mom said, "Lydia, you are welcome to use our pool anytime." Which was just my mother doing her polite thing, only Lydia took it seriously.

My dad had the pool built. It has a waterfall.

That afternoon I was still mad at Lydia. She didn't even have a clue how upset I was when she told Ms. Traison that instead of reading *Othello*, I watched the movie.

"Suki's coming over to work on our English project," I said.

The very last person I wanted to see was Lydia. But there she was with a sundress over her bathing suit and carrying her stupid *Mega Maiden Marauders* beach towel. She was the only person at school who still watched that cartoon.

"That's okay," she said. "I won't bother you."

"Really," I pressed. Seriously, the girl could not take a hint. "It might be weird with us doing homework, while you're swimming."

"It'll be okay," Lydia assured me. "I don't mind."

See. Clueless.

LYDIA CHAN

I loved hanging out with Zoe. It was super fun having the most popular girl in school as one of my best friends. Plus, she had a pool. My backyard had brown grass.

"Suki's coming over to work on our English project," Zoe said.

"That's okay," I told her. "I won't bother you."

"Really," Zoe said, looking concerned. "It might be weird with us doing homework, and you swimming."

"It'll be okay," I assured her. "I don't mind."

Zoe scowled, then her eyes lit up. "You want to try something funny?" she asked.

I was always up for fun. That's the way I roll. "Sure. What?" Zoe smiled. "Okay, here's the plan," she began.

SUKI WEINSTEIN

I really didn't want to go to Zoe Kaling's house, but we were partners on the *Othello* project for Ms. Traison's class. Zoe didn't even read the book and had bragged to everyone that instead she watched the movie starring Justin Fry, the rock rapper turned actor.

When Ms. Traison asked who had finished reading *Othello*, Zoe raised her hand, along with me and Riley Ochoa. Then Lydia Chan said, "Zoe, you didn't read it, you said you watched the movie!"

The look Zoe gave Lydia could have sliced through steel, but Lydia just smiled. I don't even think she knew that Zoe was mad at her.

LYDIA

At first I didn't want to do it, but Zoe insisted. "It'll be fun," she said. "What are you afraid of?"

"I'm not afraid," I lied. Actually that wasn't true. I'm afraid of the dark and sleep with the lights on. Last year I saw a TV show and this lady with a pinched face said there are little bugs that crawl around in the dark and bite. They're called Noseeums because *no one sees 'um*, get it? No-see-um. *Noseeum.*

"This is just for fun," Zoe said. "I'll ask Suki what she thinks of you, and after she says a bunch of nice things I'll give the signal and you burst out of the closet. It'll be like one of those prank shows."

"What if she doesn't say something nice?" I asked.

"She will."

Zoe looked like she really, really wanted to do this, and I hated to let her down. That summer when her dad left, I was always at Zoe's house, and even though she hardly talked to me, her mom said, "Thank you, Lydia. You are a true friend."

"Can I leave the door open a little bit?" I asked. The Noseeums were still crawling through my mind.

Zoe sighed. She sighed a lot. "Whatever," she said.

"Then let's do it!" I yelled to show my enthusiasm.

Zoe smiled. I think she should have won Best Smile at school, but Suki won that. Suki wins everything.

"When I say 'Jelly doughnut!' that's your cue to come out," Zoe said.

"Jelly doughnut?" I asked. "Can you say 'glazed doughnut'? I like those better."

"Fine," Zoe said, sighing again. See what I mean? "Glazed doughnut."

ZOE

"Fine," I said, sighing. "Glazed doughnut."

Lydia is unbelievable. Totally weird, like she's from another planet. She's always at my house and probably thinks she lives here. But if I asked her to go away, she'd probably have a meltdown or something. I swear she uses me. Plus, anytime

I get something new to wear, you can bet that the next week, Lydia will have an outfit just like it. How annoying is that?

LYDIA

It took a while for my eyes to adjust, but then I could see. I left the door open a tiny bit so the Noseeums wouldn't come out, and there was a sliver of light shining through.

Zoe had the best clothes. One of her dresses still had its tags on. It was from Fashion Haus, that expensive store in the mall—the one with the (fake) camel in the middle of it. I made a mental note to find a dress like that at Frick's Basement. They had the same sort of clothes, but cheaper.

SUKI

Zoe was acting sort of funny when she let me into her house, like she knew a secret. I wondered if she had heard that Lydia told Riley that I liked him. Everyone knew that Zoe liked Riley, too, but he didn't like her. He thought she was stuck-up. A lot of people did. It was sort of strange because not many people liked Zoe, but everyone was scared of her. She had a mean sense of humor and would look you right in the eyes while she was smiling and cutting you down.

"Let's do our project in my room," Zoe said.

LYDIA

I could hear them talking before they came in. *What will Suki say about me?* I wondered. Even though she's in the same grade as me and Zoe, Suki seems like she's years older. She's really nice and everyone likes her, especially Riley Ochoa. He's so cute and smart. He can do math in his head. When I told Riley that Suki liked him, he looked so happy that I felt like a million dollars. More than a million. A million and one hundred dollars!

Everyone's got a crush on Riley. Even Zoe.

ZOE

We did the usual chitchat about school and stuff, but Suki kept wanting to talk about *Othello*, which was totally boring. Then the topic of Riley Ochoa came up. I can't believe that people think he likes her. Sure, she's pretty, but she's one of those girls who likes to remind everyone that she's smart.

"What do you think of Riley?" I asked.

Suki turned red.

"He's okay," she said.

Liar. Everyone knew she had a crush on him.

"Don't worry," I told her. "When Lydia blabbed that you liked him, I told him that she's nuts and always makes up things."

This made Suki turn even redder.

"So, what do you think about Lydia?" I asked.

LYDIA

I couldn't believe that Zoe said I was nuts. That was mean.

Then Suki said, "Lydia is not responsible for her own actions. Too many iced Karamel Koffees have left her with a serious case of brain freeze."

Not nice. Not nice!

Just then I felt a pinch on my face. A Noseeum??!!!

"Mmmmoooh!" I yelped as I slapped my cheek where the bug bit me. But I was really quiet about it, especially because I wanted to hear what Suki was saying to Zoe.

ZOE

What she said about Lydia was pretty funny, but Suki stopped being funny when she started talking about me.

SUKI

"The real question should be: what do people think of you, Zoe Kaling?" I said. "Perhaps the adjectives *selfish* or *self-absorbed* come into play? You speak 'mere prattle without practice'!"

ZOE

Adjectives? And "prattle without practice"? I wasn't sure exactly what she was trying to say, but I was fairly certain it wasn't anything good.

SUKI

Why couldn't Riley have been my *Othello* partner? At least he read the book. When I quoted Shakespeare, Zoe had a blank look on her face. The one she has when she doesn't get her way. And then, when she started yelling, "Jelly doughnut! Jelly doughnut!" I knew it was time to leave.

ZOE

"Why didn't you jump out of the closet like we had planned?" I asked Lydia after Suki bolted.

LYDIA

"Because you were supposed to say 'Glazed doughnut,'" I reminded her.

Wait, was that a Noseeum crawling on me?

ZOE

I tried to ignore it when Lydia slapped herself in the face. She was always doing weird things like that. "Are you still going swimming?" I asked.

Lydia nodded. She was wearing one of my sweaters.

"I think I'll join you," I said.

Now that Suki was gone, I certainly wasn't going to work on *Othello* by myself.

SUKI

I knew from the moment I went into Zoe's room that I was being set up. I could see Lydia's *Mega Maiden Marauders* beach towel in the corner. She's the only one at school who will be seen with something like that. Plus, Zoe kept glancing toward the closet, and, at one point, I heard an odd squealing noise coming out of it.

If they wanted to know what I thought about Lydia, I'd give them a bonus and say what I thought of Zoe, as well. The thing is that Lydia is harmless. A pain, but harmless. But Zoe, well, Zoe Kaling is dangerous. She will smile as she stabs you in the back.

LYDIA

It was so fun doing laps in the pool while Zoe floated on an inflated alligator. I really liked her sunglasses, too. I think I'll get a pair like that.

"So, what do you think of Suki?" I asked.

ZOE

"I don't trust her," I told Lydia.

She insisted on doing laps, only Lydia couldn't swim straight and kept splashing me. My dad used to swim fifty laps a day. He has a pool exactly like this one at his new house, with his new family. I don't know if he still does laps.

"What do you think of Suki?" I asked.

LYDIA

"Exactly what you said," I told her. Zoe was right, as usual. That Suki Weinstein can't be trusted. "She's not a true friend."

ZOE

"You're right, Lydia," I said. Then I flipped the alligator over and dove to the bottom of the pool.

Mike Winchell

I CAN'T BELIEVE YOU DID THAT!

Being Surprised by What Some People Do

In middle school, I had a social studies teacher who didn't do things like other teachers. He had no seating chart, no homework, no rules, and no daily schedule. He wanted us to come to class every day ready for anything, and be open to whatever that class period had in store for us. And it worked. We walked through that door every day with our eyes wide open, full of electric enthusiasm about what might happen.

And that's the way life is, if you think about it. It would be boring if we knew what would happen every second of every day of our lives. There'd be no adventure because there'd be no excitement about what the future might hold for us. Because let's face it: *Anything* can happen.

Our authors have had some pretty unpredictable moments occur, too. Chris Rylander shares how he was once shocked when he was bitten—by another person. Dee Garretson tells how a seemingly useless dog took everyone by surprise. And Nathan Hale's illustrated works show us how a strange bunny-head costume led to a prank that may have gone too far.

WHAT REALLY HAPPENED

BITE OF PASSAGE

When I was in high school, I worked at two different video stores and the local movie theater in my small North Dakota hometown. It had sixteen screens and was the only theater in town. Almost every employee was either in high school or college. We usually had a lot of fun working together.

One day, a fellow employee, "Vic," came up to me as I cleaned the popcorn machine.

"Chris, there's something I need to tell you," he said, his face dark. "The other guys didn't want me to, but I think you deserve to know."

"Um, okay," I said, finding it hard to swallow all of a sudden.

"The thing is," Vic said, "if Austin bites you, you shouldn't fight back."

"What?" was all I could manage.

Austin was one of Vic's friends and a fellow employee. He had a high-school rap sheet that seemed as strangely impossible as it was impressive: starting center and one of the captains on the varsity football team, stellar grades and in the advanced track in all subjects, on Student Council, best singer in the school choir, lead chair in whatever instrument he chose in band and orchestra, and just generally very popular and likeable.

"If Austin bites you, don't fight back," Vic repeated.

"What do you mean, if Austin bites me?" I asked, sure he was messing with me now.

"Well, that's just what he does. He bites people. Girls, guys, freshman, seniors, everybody. He bites everybody. But that's not the point. The point is: When he bites you, don't fight back. Because it will only make him bite harder. Struggling only makes it worse. You can't stop him; he's basically indestructible."

I tried to ignore the fact that he'd changed his phrasing from "if he bites you" to "*when* he bites you." Instead, I tried to focus on the ridiculousness of what he was telling me.

"He bit you?" I asked.

"Of course," Vic said with a grin. "He'll get you, too. Eventually. I just wanted to let you know not to fight back when he does."

As I sat there, crouched next to the popcorn machine, watching Vic meander away while whistling the tune to one of his band's songs, all I could think was: They're messing with me. They had to be. No way was Austin going to bite me. That would be insane, right?

About two weeks later, we were cleaning the theaters between movie showtimes. I was changing the trash can in the hallway, when I heard a theater door swing shut behind me.

I turned around and saw Austin sprinting toward me down the hallway.

His long, curly hair bounced with each loping step. His eyes were so wide and crazed they pinned me down in the corner like a pair of tranquilizer darts. His mouth was already open, and I saw teeth that were impossibly huge dripping saliva onto his cheek, where it streamed back toward his neck under the sheer velocity of his approach.

He's going to bite me, I thought.

Yet I stood there and did nothing.

Before I knew it, his teeth were clamped firmly onto my right forearm. I stood and watched his head shift and bob above my arm as he attempted to get a better grip with his powerful jaws. I was in shock. How could this be happening?

I was snapped from my trance by the realization that he was biting me hard. The pain intensified to the point where it felt like he might just strip my entire arm of its skin.

I noticed I was still holding the heavy plastic and metal trash can lid in my left hand. I looked from it to Austin's head and back again. I thought of Vic's warning, but based on the pain, I didn't even think it was possible for Austin to bite harder.

I slammed the lid onto Austin's skull several times as hard as I could. The clanging impacts reverberated in the small hallway, sounding almost like gunshots.

I had been wrong: He could, and *did*, bite harder. As soon as I made contact with his head, his jaws clamped down to the point where it truly felt like my arm was going to snap in half. I ceased my defensive measures immediately.

Instead, I stamped my foot and began to whimper at the excruciating pain. I tried to wait calmly as he finished his bite. To this day, I still don't know how long a human-to-human bite should take, but in my case it was about fifteen seconds.

Austin finally released my arm and then walked away without saying a word.

I looked down and stared at my arm in shock. He had bitten me so hard it looked like a bomb exploded on my forearm. At the epicenter was the red and purple ring of his teeth, where blood slowly oozed through the broken skin. Cascading away from that were swells of purples and yellows, stretching all the way from my wrist to my elbow. In the days that followed, a hard lump developed in my arm, and the bruising intensified to where it looked like I'd actually broken my arm in half. The distinct teeth marks that lasted for almost a month were the only reminder that a single bite had caused this kind of damage.

Here's where it gets complicated: I wasn't mad at Austin. I don't know if his saliva contained some sort of calming toxin, but I simply wasn't mad at him. To this day, it's hard to figure out why. Ultimately, I think it's for the same reason that he got away with biting as many people as he did, which I came to find out later was quite a few: He was simply that strangely likeable.

Austin should have become my enemy that day, but instead he remained one of my work friends. We never really hung out much outside of work, but we generally got along well when we worked together.

Years later, things got even more complicated. I was working at a bookstore and my girlfriend's cousin showed up and told me she was engaged.

"Congrats!" I said.

"You know the guy."

"Oh, cool, who is it?" I asked.

"Austin. You used to work with him, I guess."

I gasped and looked down at my arm on instinct. I could almost see the horrible bite wound again. And now this guy was going to marry my girlfriend's cousin?

Fast-forward several years and they are married, and so are my girlfriend and I. Which means I'm now officially related to Austin. I see him almost every Christmas at family gatherings. He has three daughters of his own now, each as insanely smart and intense and weird as he is. Which is mostly why I love hanging out with them.

I still remember the first time I told that story to his wife. She could hardly believe it. The funny thing is, to this day, he hasn't been able to offer me an explanation for why he did it. Every time I ask him about it, his response is always the same.

He laughs. Then grins. Then shrugs.

And I don't think I'd want it to be any other way.

PARKER KELLOGG'S HUGE BRAIN

Wilson always was a weird kid. Everybody at Samuel Ireland Middle School knew that. From the way he always wore sandals, even in the dead of winter, to his choice of pairing running shorts with giant wool cardigan sweaters, to the frequent sweatbands that hugged his stringy hair to his large forehead, we'd all known he was a little off ever since grade school.

It's partly why I like him so much. He has the guts to be who he wants to be, regardless of what people think of him.

It's not just the way he dresses—his penchant for carrying around his schoolbooks and notebooks in old plastic grocery bags doesn't help. Plus, there is the constant snacking on animal crackers, and his inability to hold a regular conversation for more than ten minutes without eventually breaking topic and asking something like, "Do you guys ever wonder how people first realized that other animals were edible? Like, was it an accident or did some caveman just consciously decide to eat his pet pig one day? And, what stopped them from drawing the line at animals and not eventually start eating each other?"

You never knew whether he was trying to make us laugh or not, he never lets anyone in on the joke—if he's joking at all, that is.

The point is this: We all knew he was a little off. But somehow, he still always found a way to surprise me. To show me a new side of him that I never even knew existed.

It's a Thursday about as normal as any other Thursday. Which means my day starts at 7:50 in the morning with homeroom. And the first time I see Wilson will be at lunch, where we'll get baked chicken and creamed corn and a hunk of white stuff that supposedly moonlights as bread, just like every other third Thursday of the month.

At lunchtime, I get my food and sit down next to Wilson like always. He usually greets me on chicken day by saluting with a drumstick. Today, however, he merely sits there and looks at the chicken on his plate, as if he's waiting to have a conversation with it about something important.

Wilson is wearing a gray sweatshirt with a huge and bright horse print on it. He found it at the Salvation Army that summer; I was with him at the time. He picks out secondhand clothes with a sort of deliberate calm that always makes me wonder if he selects such things ironically or just simply enjoys rescuing discarded items from certain death. This is another reason I like Wilson; he's like a walking mystery novel, and no matter how many pages you tear through, you never seem to get any real answers. He's infinitely engrossing.

"What's up," I say, sitting down. "Staring contest with your chicken?"

"Hmmm?" he says without looking up.

"What's with you?" I ask. He is acting even stranger than usual.

"Oh, sorry," he finally says, looking up at me.

His eyes are red and sunken into purple sockets. He looks half dead. Wilson is always a little pale and had always looked just a few years from death ever since we became friends in third grade. But he looks especially awful today, even for him.

"What happened to you?" I ask.

"I didn't sleep well," he says. "This homeless guy last night . . . it was weird."

"What?" I say. "This homeless guy, what?"

"Oh, it was nothing," Wilson says. "I was walking home through the park and he attacked me. I mean, I got away, but it was weird."

He shrugs a single shoulder slowly, as if stretching it out, and then grimaces in pain.

"Oh, man, seriously?" I say.

"It's fine," he mumbles.

But I notice that he's staring at my arm now. Not just looking at my arm, but staring *into* it. Like he's in some sort of trance. I want to slide slowly away, but I'm too intrigued to move.

Before I know what's even happening, Wilson lunges at me. He grabs me and locks his teeth on to my forearm. At first, I almost laugh; in fact, I think I do let out a few guffaws. Then, when I realize how hard he is biting me, it turns into a cry of pain.

I stand up, trying to pull away from my friend. But his teeth are clamped on to my arm like a vise. Struggling with him is only making the pain worse.

So I sit back down, trying to keep from screaming, even as all the other kids around us make no such effort. They're all yelling and shouting, some even laughing, but I barely hear any of it. I'm still in shock.

"Wilson," I finally say, "what are you doing?"

He replies only with a weird guttural growl and then repositions his jaws to bite me even harder.

"Stop it, dude!" I shout.

There are two teachers around us now and they somehow manage to pry Wilson away from me. As soon as they get his jaws detached from my throbbing forearm, he slumps to the floor in a sitting position. His eyes are open and he is awake, but he looks totally lost, gazing around as if he just woke up.

"Whoa, did I do that?" he asks, pointing at my arm.

I'm almost afraid to look, but eventually force myself to. Then I immediately wish I hadn't. Chunks of skin are pushed aside and blood slowly oozes from two semicircle-shaped gashes opposite each other. The wound has already started bruising.

"What was that all about?" I ask him, cradling my arm, as the two lunchroom chaperones lift him to his feet.

My arm feels like it's on fire. Or, no, that doesn't quite do it justice. It actually feels like someone first pounded the dull, metal leg to one of the cafeteria chairs into my forearm with a baseball bat, drenched it in lighter fluid, and *then* set it ablaze. It's all at once burning and throbbing and stinging sharply.

"Let me see that," a third teacher, Mrs. Orwell, says to me.

I hold out my arm, still staring in disbelief at Wilson.

"I don't know," he says, shaking his head. "I don't know, I just wanted a bite."

Then he is being led away. I watch him shuffle out of the cafeteria with the two teachers at his side.

"We'd better get you to the nurse," Mrs. Orwell says to me.

★ ★ ★

Wilson is not at school the next day. But the whole school is talking about him. They whisper as I pass in the hallways that morning, staring at my bandaged arm.

I didn't need stitches or anything. But I will be taking Tylenol all day. The constant throbbing in my arm is offset only by the sharp, stabbing pain anytime something even so much as brushes against my bandages.

I'm blaming the odd light-headedness I feel on the pain.

After taking my seat in homeroom, I concentrate on the back of Dallas Walter's gigantic head. His noggin is enormous. A lot of kids at school call him D. W. Bighead. He's not particularly fond of the nickname, but he rolls with it because he'd probably get called that even more if kids knew it bothered him.

I'm staring at it just to try to distract myself from all the other kids staring at me, the one kids are calling simply: *Biting Victim*. It's not that often that horrific biting attacks break out during lunch in middle school. Elementary school? Maybe. But not during seventh-grade lunch, no way. That's just plain weird.

The funny thing, after staring at Dallas's planetary melon for fifteen minutes, is that I can't help but wonder how big his brain is. Like, is his brain proportionately massive? Or is it normal size and he just has a thicker skull than most people? I don't know, but I find myself rooting for the Giant Brain possibility. It seems more refreshing, somehow.

Maybe he's telepathic? Maybe his deliciously monstrous brain has parts to it that other people's don't have. I don't know if that could possibly be true, but it's a tasty possibility regardless.

By the end of class, I'm half tempted to try to bite open his head to find out. Unfortunately, the pain in my arm distracts me enough to allow him to get up and out of class before I even realize that the bell has rung.

I hurry out of the room and into the throng of kids in the hallway, barely able to walk amid the excruciating pain. I go to the nearest bathroom and slowly lift my bandage in front of the mirror. I'm not sure what I expect to see, but I gasp when I finally see the wound.

It's green and yellow and seems to be oozing and pulsating as if it were alive. It's gross, but the sight of it almost seems to dull the pain somehow. Is this what bite-wound infections normally look like? I have no idea. But removing the bandage seems to have helped with the pain somehow, so I toss the gooey mess into the trash and pull down the sleeves of my sweatshirt.

I head to second period math class.

★ ★ ★

Halfway into second period, my stomach rumbles loud enough to turn a few heads. I shrug at Freddy K., the kid sitting next to me. He smirks back.

"Skip breakfast?" he asks.

"No, but maybe the Tylenol is making me extra hungry."

He just shakes his head. I wonder how much brain is sloshing around inside his skull. It seems like an odd thing to think about. Maybe my arm is infected and I'm getting a fever?

I look straight ahead and try to ignore the twisting of my empty stomach.

I never noticed before now just how huge Parker Kellogg's head is. I'm starting to feel like the entire school is jam-packed with huge-headed mutants. His skull is so massive that his hair hangs across it in stringy blond strips like shreds of lettuce.

My stomach rumbles again.

Parker turns around, placing a meaty shank of an arm onto my desk.

"Dude, what's with all the noises?" he asks.

I'm really not sure why I do what I do next. But I can't help myself. I lunge forward and clamp my teeth on to his bicep. As soon as I feel his soft skin in my jaws, I just want to bite harder. It's like I no longer can control my own actions, as I try to tear the whole muscle away from his arm.

Parker screams and then suddenly I am vaguely aware of being pulled away by the teacher.

The class is in chaos; I see kids' shocked faces staring at me. Except I don't really see faces, but just shells containing delicious snacks. Like peanut shells. Peanut shells with eyeballs.

Then I'm being marched down to the principal's office by the teacher, Mr. Donner. He is talking, but I can't make out what he is saying. All I can think about is how big his brain must be given his ability to crunch numbers in his head so quickly, as he often demonstrates for us in class.

Then I'm seated at the principal's desk. Her huge brain hovers above me, pulsing with activity.

She's droning on and on about a rash of biting attacks at the school and demands to know the meaning of it all.

I hear myself groan in reply.

I was trying to tell her that *I got bit, too, you know. It's not all my fault.*

So, I try to speak again, to clarify myself.

"Agggghhhhrrrhggg," I say. "Uhhhhng."

That didn't sound right. I know this. I try again, as I stand up and lunge across the desk at her.

"Braiiiiins!" I say.

That's closer to what I'm trying to say. I know this, since it was at least an actual word. Much closer to what I want.

Principals are smart. They have huge brains. Huge, delicious brains. Brainy brains.

She shoves me away, and out her window I see Wilson

chasing a kid across the parking lot. Wilson looks awful. His normally pale skin has gone completely pasty gray, like a slab of concrete.

I root for Wilson to catch the kid. To catch him and get his delicious brains.

Brains would taste so good.

I know this.

Brains are so tasty. It's a fact I am suddenly aware of and surprised I never knew before. Brainy brains are the tastiest.

"Braaaiiins," I hear myself say. "Brains, braiiins, braiiiiinsssss."

The brainsipal screams.

She brains away from my brains to get brains brains.

Brains are brains and brainy, brain brained brains.

Brains.

Braaaaaaaaainss.

A DOG NAMED KITTY

My sister deserves the blame for the dog's name. Even though I picked out the puppy, the liveliest one in the litter, my older sister won the name game. She thought it would be funny to call "Here, Kitty!" and when a dog came running people would laugh. It might have been funny if Kitty had ever learned to come when called. She didn't. In fact, she never learned anything remotely resembling good dog behavior.

Kitty started off with one big disadvantage. Our previous pet had been a wonder dog named Queenie, who set a high standard for all the pets that followed. Queenie knew actual dog tricks, lots of them. Kitty, on the other hand, couldn't begin to do a trick. She'd look at me with a puzzled expression when I'd try to teach her to sit or shake hands or play dead. I like to think she just decided it was silly to do such things, though I suspect it was actually a distinct lack of doggy intelligence.

Not only did Kitty fail in the trick category, she also had

an annoying habit of barking at imaginary things. Most dogs bark at strangers or squirrels or other dogs. Kitty ignored all those. Instead, we'd find her standing in the middle of the room barking fiercely at some terrible thing in front of her that only she could see. She also chewed up everything. No shoe was safe. This did not endear her to my mother, who loved shoes far more than animals. If one of her shoes fell victim, my mother would take a broom after the dog and banish her to the garage.

Kitty's worst offense occurred one Christmas Eve. My mother liked to do themed Christmas trees, and one year she decorated the whole tree in cardinals and red bows. It took her a long time to get the ornaments in just the right places, and she was very pleased with the end result. Kitty lay nearby, her eyes tracking each ornament placement. Later that night, I should have been suspicious when she didn't follow me into my room to sleep.

I got up early Christmas morning to discover what had occupied her during the night. Red feathers and bits of plastic birds covered the floor. Though Kitty couldn't do a regular dog trick, she'd apparently mastered leaping up in the air and nabbing the birds off the tree. Banished yet again to the garage, Kitty spent the day barking at imaginary garage invaders, not realizing she was skirting close to a drastic banishment, a permanent one.

Kitty's happier times were spent at our cabin by the lake. My mother didn't come there often, and even when she did, there wasn't a garage. Kitty loved riding in the boat and swimming in the lake with us. There also seemed to be fewer imaginary invaders. The cabin wasn't fancy. Most of it was just one big room. At night we'd lay out sleeping bags on the floor, wherever there was space, and listen to the crickets until we fell asleep. Kitty would curl up at the end of my sleeping bag and doze, occasionally growling in her dreams.

One ordinary night, we were jolted awake by Kitty's frantic barking. My father yelled at her to be quiet, but she wouldn't. Grumbling, he turned on the light. Kitty grew more frantic, barking hysterically at my sister's sleeping bag. My sister, not a cheerful person when woken in the night, added her voice to the yelling, but Kitty continued to bark. When I went to grab the dog's collar, I noticed something small scurry under the sleeping bag.

My father flipped up the end to reveal a scorpion, the nasty stinging insect we feared but rarely saw. We knew a sting could result in a trip to the hospital, so we were always careful out-side, but it had never occurred to us one could get inside to crawl around the sleeping bags. My father disposed of the invader. My sister was saved. Kitty was hailed as a hero dog, taking her place in our family history alongside Queenie, the wonder dog.

After that, Kitty still barked at nothing and chewed up shoes, but her place with us was secure. I made her a bed for the times she spent in the garage, and dragged a chair out to keep her company. I think she appreciated the companionship, sure that the two of us would be more than enough to keep those invisible intruders pinned down in the garage and out of the house.

Dee Garretson

DART THE DRAGON HOUND

Piggy whined at the red sky swirling over the wastelands to the south of the castle, and then slunk down low to crawl behind the woodpile, so only his nose and his front paws were visible.

"Silly dog," I said. "The sky can't hurt you."

One of the cooks came out of the kitchen. "Rowan, when you're done sweeping the yard, we need more wood inside." She glanced at the sky and made a sign against evil. "Nothing can burn like that for so many months."

Piggy whined again, and the cook peered around trying to spot him. "Don't let that pest of a dog in when you bring the wood. He gets underfoot."

"I won't," I promised. I kept Piggy close to me so he'd not run afoul of my grandfather, the king's kennel master.

"I should have drowned that dog when it was a pup," he'd mutter every time he saw Piggy. "The runt of the litter is never any good, and that dog is proof. Barking at nothing, chasing its own tail, chewing on everything. It's worthless."

Since my brothers call me the runt of the litter, too, born the smallest of us and with one leg shorter than the other, I always tried to defend Piggy, but my grandfather would just frown and stomp away.

Piggy couldn't get into too much trouble under the wood rack, so I left him there and went back to sweeping. A chattering of girls' voices from behind the gate warned me the princess and her horde of ladies-in-waiting were about to invade the yard. Before I could disappear, the princess spotted me.

"Rowan, where's my little piggy?" she called as she dashed out the gate. She stopped in the middle of the yard and spun around, her arms raised high and her head flung back, making her long brown hair swirl. Every time she came outside, she did that, as if being let free.

I ducked my head and managed to choke out a few words. "He's under the woodpile, my lady." I wanted to kick myself for not being able to speak up in her presence, but the sight of the princess always made me feel awkward and tongue-tied.

"Here little piggy, piggy," she crooned as she went over to the woodpile.

Immediately, Piggy crawled out on his belly, wagging his tail. He loved the princess, though she only remembered his existence once in a while.

"That's not a pig," a tall girl said. "That's a dog."

I didn't recognize this one, who had a pinched look to her face, but since the ladies-in-waiting came and went on some schedule I didn't understand, it wasn't surprising that I'd never seen her before.

"He was a little piggy when he was a puppy," the princess said. "He'd climb right in the middle of the food bowl and gobble down all the food he could before the bigger puppies got it all. I gave him his name. Isn't he adorable? Just like a little black piglet."

No one answered right away, though I knew what they were thinking. Piggy was anything but adorable. His legs had never grown long like the other hunting dogs, and while he was not exactly fat, he was far more round in the belly than the other dogs since he didn't go hunting.

"Rowan, have you taught him any tricks yet?" the princess asked.

I wanted to disappear under the woodpile myself. "I'm teaching him to fetch," I mumbled. I didn't add that the lessons weren't going well. I'd throw a stick and Piggy would just sit beside me, his head tipped to the side, like he was wondering when I was going to retrieve the stick I'd just thrown.

"My father says dogs should be useful or they aren't worth keeping," the pinched-face girl said. "Fetching isn't useful."

"He did catch a snake," I said. It had surprised both Piggy and me when he'd pounced on the thing as it slithered across the keep. I doubted the dog had ever seen one before. Snakes were rare in the north.

The princess looked impressed, though the rest of the girls

did not. She started to speak, but a low rumble from the south distracted her.

The red in the sky had darkened, more like the color of blood now. A shiver ran down my back.

"It's getting closer," the princess whispered. "The air smells strange, like something foul is burning."

One of the smaller girls asked, "What do you think the sky means? What could burn for so long?"

The girl next to her said, "My mother thinks it's a big volcano. I hope the lava doesn't cover us all up."

The tall girl said, "My father believes it's a dragon storm. The dragons come from the south and burn the land until there is nothing left."

"There haven't been dragons for thousands of years, not even in the south," the princess said. "It's probably just a dust storm."

Piggy chose that moment to have one of his barking fits. No one knew what set them off, but Piggy would go into a flurry of movement, twisting around and barking hysterically, but always at nothing anyone else could see.

"Silly dog!" The princess clapped her hands and laughed as if Piggy were putting on a show. I could see the dog trembling, though, like he was terrified of something. I wished I knew how to stop him.

Finally, Piggy exhausted himself and collapsed on the ground. We all stood there looking at the dog until a bell sounded in the chapel.

"We have to go, Rowan," the princess said, "but you'll give poor little Piggy some water, won't you? He looks thirsty." She gathered up her skirts and headed back in through the door, the ladies-in-waiting following.

"That dog is an embarrassment to the king." My grandfather's deep voice came from behind me. "It's time to be rid of it."

As if he understood, Piggy slunk back under the wood rack.

"No! The king hasn't ever seen Piggy act like that. And anyway, the princess likes Piggy. She thinks he's her dog."

Grandfather snorted. "She'd forget about him the moment he was gone, just like any trinket of hers. Royalty has too much of everything to care about any one thing. Next time she's off on a visit somewhere, the dog goes." He walked away.

I wanted to yell after him, but I didn't. Grandfather had a heavy hand when he was angered. Besides, he'd never change his mind. I felt sick at the thought of what was going to happen.

Piggy crawled back out and pushed his nose into my hand, the heat radiating off his skin like he was burning up. "Let's get you some water," I said, determined not to cry.

The next morning Piggy took up a spot on the far side of the yard, staring at the sky to the south. He wouldn't even eat the bun I tried to share with him, so I took up my morning chores.

Before I got very far, my grandfather found me. "I need you to come with me today to help with the dogs. The king wants to hunt, and that fool of a helper of mine broke his leg last night climbing a wall to impress a girl." He shook his head in disgust. "A few of the younger dogs are going out for the first time today, and if they don't behave, I want you to bring them back."

"Yes, sir," I said, glancing over at Piggy. I hoped the dog wouldn't try to follow, but I didn't need to worry. Piggy didn't seem to notice when I left, too busy watching the sky.

In the kennel yard, the excited dogs milled about, though they quieted at the sight of my grandfather. He stooped down to pick something up and I saw his whip on the ground instead of on its usual hook. Some dog, Piggy most likely, had pulled it off its hook and chewed it in two.

When grandfather stood back up, his face was as red as the sky. "That mutt goes in the river the minute we get back."

I didn't let my grandfather see the panic his words caused me. All sorts of ideas jumped into my head. Piggy and I could run away. I could find a job in a village somewhere, working in a livery stable, or helping out at an inn. There was no way I'd let Piggy be drowned. During the hunt, I vowed I'd make a plan.

I was surprised to see the princess on her pony, accompanied by a few of her ladies on theirs. She even had her bow and arrow with her, though it was so small it was more like a child's toy rather than a real weapon.

"Papa, should we really go south?" the princess asked her father. "Some of the girls are frightened of the sky."

"Don't worry," the king said. "The scouts I sent out reported nothing unusual."

His words assured the princess, who smiled and signaled her ladies to follow her, but I wasn't so sure. It didn't matter what I thought, though. We set off, walking behind the hunters for a time until the hunt master signaled for silence. A stag stood on top of a nearby hill. The king rode forward, followed by the rest of the hunters.

Just as the king raised his bow, a dog barked, alerting the stag, who leaped away. I cringed. I hadn't seen Piggy come up behind us. He stood and continued to bark, louder than I'd ever heard him, facing the south, eyes poised on the red sky. I tried to move between Piggy and my grandfather as my grandfather ran forward, but I couldn't get there in time. He kicked the dog in the side. Piggy's body flew up in the air and landed hard.

The king's face was thunderous as he turned back. He drew closer and stared down at Piggy, who lay in the dirt. I prayed the dog was still breathing, though if he was, I didn't know what my grandfather would do. "Kennel master," the king's voice boomed, "where did this dog come from?"

"Sire!" one of the hunters shouted. "Look above!"

A black cloud bore down on us, a swirling mass of flying creatures.

"Is it dragons?" someone yelled.

"Too small for dragons," the king said. "It looks just like some kind of big black birds."

There were nervous laughs from the group, but then a terrible choking stench filled the air.

"I'm not sure those are birds," the princess said.

We all froze as the flock passed over us. One of the creatures veered out and dove down, landing right next to the king.

133

"What . . . what is it?" someone asked.

The thing before us looked a bit like an image of a dragon I'd seen once on a banner, but it was only the size of a very large, skinny bird. It seemed more like a snake with wings and legs than some legendary creature. The thing's head swung back and forth, its yellow eyes fixed on the king. A squawk came from it, like a chicken, though no chicken ever smelled so bad.

"So much for a fearsome dragon." The king laughed and dismounted from his horse, drawing his sword.

The dragon opened his mouth, and an enormous blast of fire shot forth, engulfing the king. The scene turned to chaos as horses bolted in every direction. Some of the men surrounded the king, beating at the flames. The dogs fled even though my grandfather shouted at them to stay. The princess tried to get her pony under control, but the animal was frantic. It took off running, the princess clinging to the reins.

The creature took to the air again and I saw it was heading in the same direction as the princess. I ran after them, cursing my too-short leg, which slowed me down.

The dragon caught up to the pony, circling overhead. The pony stumbled, nearly going down. It recovered, but then stumbled again, its legs quivering. I could see it had gone lame.

The dragon landed, only feet away from the princess. Throwing herself off her pony, the princess positioned herself between it and the dragon, like she was going to protect the animal from the dragon's fire. She pulled her bow off the saddle and grabbed an arrow out of the quiver.

"No!" I shouted. Even if that little arrow hit, it would only anger the creature.

I didn't realize Piggy had followed me until he came around from behind me and lunged at the creature, grabbing it by its neck. The dragon struggled, and its tail lashed about, hitting Piggy hard in the side, but the dog didn't let go. I leaped forward and grabbed the end of the tail, nearly dropping it as I felt it burn my palm. I hung on, hoping one of the hunters would come to help.

The princess raised her bow and took aim. I closed my eyes and held my breath, thinking the arrow would surely hit Piggy or me. Time stood still.

The dragon's tail went limp in my grasp. I exhaled.

"You can open your eyes, Rowan," the princess said. The creature was dead, an arrow piercing its throat. I dropped the tail as people ran up and surrounded us.

Piggy was the hero of the day, though I got my share of the attention, too. The king turned out to have only minor burns, his heavy leather jerkin and leggings protecting him from the worst of the dragon flame. His beard and his eyebrows suffered the most damage, but they soon grew back.

My grandfather had the sense to take the stinking carcass back to the castle, using it to train some of the braver dogs as dragon hunters. I helped him.

When the dragons came back, we were ready. Piggy would always be the canine hunt master, dancing and circling around the creatures that landed. He'd wait for just the right moment and then dart in for the attack, pinning down the beast until one of the hunters could kill it. Then he'd move on to the next dragon, quickly darting after it and pinning it down. He was relentless in his dart-and-tackle method of dragon hunting.

The princess renamed him Dart the Dragon Hound for his exploits. He got to sit at her feet in the great hall during dinner, eating the tidbits she fed him, though he still kept me company the rest of the time. He and I moved into a loft above the kennels, where I took over as assistant kennel master.

Piggy never did learn any regular dog tricks, but he didn't need them. Taking down dragons was the best trick of all.

WHEN I WAS TWELVE, MY SIBLINGS AND I FOUND A FIBERGLASS BUNNY HEAD IN OUR BASEMENT.

WHAT'S THIS!?

AAAAGH!

MY GRANDPARENTS OWNED AND OPERATED A LARGE COMMUNITY THEATER. OUR BASEMENT WAS OFTEN USED TO STORE LARGE BOXES, PROPS, AND STAGE FURNITURE.

IT'S A BUNNYHEAD!

NO, IT'S A GOPHER.

IT'S A BUNNY. LOOK, THE EARS ARE BROKEN.

WHERE'S ITS FUR?

IT LOOKS BURNT.

OUR BASEMENT WAS USUALLY THE LAST STOP BEFORE THE PROP WAS THROWN AWAY.

I DON'T RECALL ANYTHING THAT WE STORED EVER GOING BACK OUT ON STAGE.

AAAAAGHHH

NONE OF US HAD EVER SEEN OUR SISTER SO SCARED. HER PANIC WAS SO TOTAL THAT WE COULDN'T HELP LAUGHING.

HA HA HA HA HA HA HA HA HA HA HA HA

LAYNA, COME DOWN. IT'S JUST A MASK.

NO! NO! NO! NO!

WE CAN BRING IT UPSTAIRS TO SHOW YOU.

NOOOOOOOO!

GO UP AND SCARE HER.

HERE IT COMES!

HERE COMES THE BUNNYHEAD!

HAHAHAHA!

MY BROTHER'S VOICE WAS STRANGE AND ECHO-Y FROM INSIDE THE HEAD. I FOUND I WANTED TO TRY IT ON, MYSELF.

GIVE ME THAT.

THE FEELING OF PUTTING ON THE BUNNYHEAD WAS VERY STRANGE.

THE INTERIOR WAS SHINY, WARPED, AND SMOOTH.

THE EYEHOLES WERE COVERED WITH SOME SORT OF MESH SCREEN THAT WAS HARD TO SEE THROUGH.

IT WAS HEAVY, AND HAD A DUSTY CHEMICAL SMELL.

LAYNAAAAAAAAAAA.

MY VOICE WAS VERY LOUD ON THE INSIDE.

LAYNAAAAAAAA!

MY PARENTS, WHO WEREN'T HOME WHEN WE FOUND THE HEAD, WERE ONLY CONFUSED BY THE STORY. TOO BAFFLED TO PUNISH US FOR THE EPISODE.

WE HAVE A BUNNY HEAD IN THE BASEMENT?

GO GET IT.

NOOOO!!

OKAY, NEVER MIND. DON'T GET IT.

FOR WEEKS AFTERWARD, WE USED THE THREAT OF THE BUNNYHEAD TO CONTROL OUR SISTER.

GO GET ME A POPSICLE OR I'LL PUT ON THE BUNNYHEAD.

NONE OF US EVER ACTUALLY PUT THE THING ON AGAIN; THE THREAT WAS ENOUGH.

IT HAD BECOME TOO POWERFUL, IT SCARED HER SO MUCH, IT SCARED US.

ONE DAY,
THE BUNNYHEAD
DISAPPEARED.

I CAN ONLY ASSUME MY PARENTS
THREW IT OUT, TIRED OF THE NONSTOP
BUNNYHEAD TALK.

I RECENTLY CALLED LAYNA TO ASK HER
WHAT SHE REMEMBERED ABOUT
THE BUNNYHEAD.

SHE LAUGHED,
BUT THERE WAS A SHIVER IN IT.
SHE TOLD ME SHE AVOIDED GOING
INTO THE BASEMENT FOR
YEARS AFTERWARD.

HAHAHAHAHAHA

WHAT I RECALL MOST CLEARLY
IS THE FEELING OF WEARING THE THING—
THE SMELL OF IT, THE *POWER* OF IT.

LOOKING OUT FROM ITS EYES, I KNEW I COULD
SCARE THE LIFE OUT OF MY SISTER. I KNEW I COULD
CONTROL HER COMPLETELY, THROUGH FEAR.

I DON'T EVER WANT TO
FEEL THAT POWER AGAIN.

I STAY AWAY FROM
BUNNYHEADS THESE DAYS.

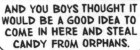

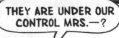

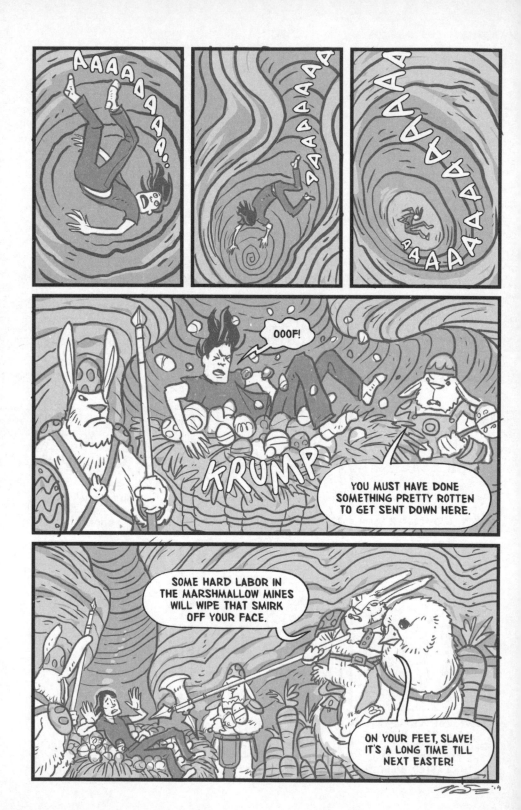

Mike Winchell

SACRIFICE

Putting
Others First

When I was young, family was my whole world. Sure, my toys were also pretty important to me at the time, but really my brothers and my parents were everything. I did whatever I could to please them. Then when middle school started, that changed. Friends became my highest priority. Family was still important, but my day-to-day life revolved around friends. When I started playing sports, my teammates became both friends *and* family all at once. All I wanted to do was *not* let my teammates down. And in all of these relationships, there were times when I thought more about my peers than I did of myself, and I sacrificed for them.

Author Matthew J. Kirby writes about a boy who puts his family and his village above his own safety. Tracy Edward Wymer shows how far baseball players will go for the sake of their team. And mother and daughter writing team Jane Yolen and Heidi E. Y. Stemple paint a picture of a family that bands together during a time of crisis.

Matthew J. Kirby

THE GARDEN

grab the weed all the way around, gathering its spreading shoots into my gloved hand so I can tug it out by the roots. When I don't, and snap them off at the stalk, they leak a sticky milk. But the recent rains have softened the ground, so most of the weeds come out easy, and the air smells like wet earth. The hot sun burns the back of my neck as I hunch over this section of overgrown, neglected yard.

We moved in a few weeks ago, and it doesn't seem the previous owners cared much about gardening. I'm not much of a gardener, either. I mean, I know plants need to be watered, or they die. Beyond that, no one would mistake my thumb for a green one.

But this matters to me now, more than it used to.

Since before I was born, my grandma had a garden. A large garden that took up about the same amount of land as her large house. A gravel road bound by railroad ties ran the length of the garden's eastern edge, separating it from the yard. Rosebushes lined this road, each a different color, each bearing

161

a different fragrance. Some of the varieties had come from the Middle East. Others from England. My grandma knew them all by name and origin: Fantin-Latour, Autumn Damask, Salet, The Fairy.

As a kid, I used to help my grandma weed, along with my siblings and cousins. She bobbed alongside us, wearing her very wide-brimmed straw hat and a long-sleeved white cotton shirt to protect her from the sun, as we moved down the rows of carrots, pumpkins, tomatoes, and everything else she grew. Sometimes, she planted corn, and let me tell you, there is nothing like sneaking a sun-warmed sweet ear and eating it raw, right there among the tall stalks.

The vegetables, berries, and fruit took up about half the garden plot. The rest belonged to the flowers, an endless array of color, shape, and size that grew thick with perfume and bumblebees. A little stone path wandered among the beds to a far corner, a secret place where my grandma had a swing and a wooden trellis.

I sometimes sat with her there in the evening light. I remember her well-worn hands, somehow tough and elegant at the same time, and her laugh that today echoes like music in my memories. She knew her plants like she knew her neighbors and lifelong friends, their histories and personalities. Here was a woman who, when I didn't know whether a plant was a weed to pull or something to leave in the ground, told me to taste it, which she did when I hesitated. Her connection to her garden took in all of her senses, along with a kind of deeper understanding that remains a mystery to me.

But time passes. Plants grow and die. My grandma aged.

She had always been a bit eccentric to me with her quirks and obsessions—her many antiques arranged just so, her daily journals, and I think she gave me the same potpourri-making lesson half a dozen times over the years—but as I grew into an adult I realized that her eccentricity disguised an undergrowth of disordered thought that gradually took over the garden of her mind.

Outside, among her vegetables and flowers, plants even I knew to be weeds crept in and were allowed to remain. My grandma's faithful watering routine faltered, leaving some plants to wither in the hot Utah sun. Flowers and bushes spilled out of their boundaries, and over time the garden took on a wild, unkempt quality that mirrored what was happening inside its gardener.

Eventually, it became apparent my grandma could no longer live on her own, and we moved her out of her house. I was able to take one last walk through the tangle of her former flower beds. I made my way to the far corner with the swing, the wooden trellis sagging nearby, and surveyed what remained.

It was somehow still the garden I remembered, but changed by the passage of years and the toll of age. Within the overgrowth I caught glimpses here and there of what used to be, hints and memories of former splendor, and in that unruliness a quiet beauty remained, persistent, perhaps even stubborn, and enduring, the essence of who my grandmother was, and is, and always will be to me.

It worried me to think of a stranger moving in, and what they might do with her garden. Would they restore it and cultivate it? Would they have a secret corner where they might sit in the evening? Or would they dig everything up and lay sod? As I left my grandma's house that day, I decided that I didn't actually want to know the answer.

Now I kneel in the dirt in my own, much smaller yard, pulling weeds, remembering. I don't know that I have any particular vision for this spot of earth. Perhaps I'll just plant a few flowers, or some herbs, like basil and parsley. But I think I'd like to do something with it.

This matters to me now, more than it used to.

Matthew J. Kirby

THE WOMAN AT THE TOP OF THE WORLD

The irony of Able's name was not lost on him, nor was it lost on his parents who had named him. But his mum and da had known at the moment of Able's birth, as soon as they had seen the little twig that was his right leg, that Able was lame and would be for the rest of his life. His parents had known what that life would be, what it would mean for their farm and in their village. They had used his name to love him, anyway.

But all his name did was remind Able of what he wasn't, and now that he was fourteen, the other boys his age in the village had years ago gone out into the fields and pastures to labor alongside the men, while Able watched from the edge of things.

"Give me a hand with this, would you, son?" his mum asked at the height of summer, her back bent over the large black kettle she kept near the fireplace, a few of her gray hairs straying from their braid.

Able hobbled over to her without a word, braced himself

against the stone chimney, and lifted the heavy kettle onto the pothook with ease.

"So strong, those hands of yours." His mum rubbed his shoulder. "And those arms. Thank you."

Able said nothing. Low voices spilled in through the open front door, and Able turned as a group of young men trudged along the lane, tools and lunch pails hanging low. He watched them pass and watched the empty road long after they'd gone.

"Even were you with them," his mum said, "there'd be no work for you. This drought has made sure of that."

Able looked down at his useless leg.

His mum gave his shoulder another rub. "I know, son, I know."

Later that evening, his da came home with shoulders hunched, wearing a grim frown. "It's all gone. Dried up."

Able's mum dropped her wooden ladle. "The north field, by the stream?"

"No more stream," his da said.

And nothing else was said that night.

The next morning, for the first time in Able's life, his da stayed at the table after he'd eaten his breakfast. No need to walk his land. Over the past two months, he'd watched his crops dry up row by row, acre by acre, and now he sat there watching nothing.

"What about the witch?" Able's mum finally asked. "Could she—"

"Three fools have gone up the mountain." His da never lifted his eyes. "None reached the peak, and all three came back empty-handed. Besides, no one has seen that old woman in years."

Able had never seen her, but he had heard the stories. Many had gone up the mountain, but few had touched the summit. Some had gone up looking for a cure, while others had gone up looking for an answer. Those who reached the witch always came away with what they sought. When he was younger, and more foolish, Able had thought about making his own pilgrimage, for his shriveled leg.

But the mountain was high, and those were just stories.

His da shook his head. "That old hag is long dead. She must be."

Yet desperate men from the village had gone up looking for an end to the drought. Perhaps there were times when belief in a story was no longer a choice, and everyone became a fool.

Able's mum walked to the table, hugging herself. "What will we do?"

His da rose from the table and took over the hugging of her. "We must prepare. There's talk in the village of combining food stores for those who choose to stay, to make sure no one starves."

Able's mum looked up from within his da's arms. "Will we stay?"

"I don't know where we would go," his da said.

They went to bed, but Able slept little, and when he did, he dreamed of shrouded mountain peaks and bony fingers. When dawn broke, and his father slept on, Able knew what he would do. He rose from his bed, dressed in silence, and left his house behind in the warm, dry morning.

The best road to the mountain cut through the heart of the village. If there had been another way he would have taken it, but the other roads would waste both time and distance, and he needed all his strength in reserve for the climb.

Men milled about the green and loitered in the streets. They all fell silent as Able hobbled past them, eyeing sidelong his crutch and his limp with familiar fear and hatred.

"Somehow, this is your fault," a man growled. "Curses beget curses."

Able brushed by him, staring straight ahead, but braced himself.

"You!" the shout came from behind him. "Curses beget curses!" But all that fell on Able's back were words.

Moments later, the village lay behind him, and his heart calmed. But then he saw the state of the land and the devastation wrought by the drought. For the next few miles, all was dead, acre after acre caked with cracked earth, prickly with the dried stubble of former crops, nothing left even for the birds. A dry wind set the dust dancing.

Able pressed forward, but very soon felt the first discomfort in his leg, a dull ache of protest at being asked to do more than it was ever meant to. The pain grew worse when he reached the edge of the last field and the road inclined upward into the foothills. The pastures there were empty of anything living. All that remained were the stone fences and the occasional skeleton of a sheep or cow draped in its sun-dried hide.

Beyond the pastures, the road climbed higher until it met the first trees and thinned to a trail, then a path. The trees were mostly pine, many no more than standing tinder waiting for an errant flame, their fragrance all dried out. Able crossed several empty streambeds, their backbones of stone laid bare, and still he labored upward.

The stress to his leg had become excruciating, the sweat on his brow as much from the pain as the heat. He had to stop often to sit and take the burden from those frail joints. His hip hurt the most. The bones there had never fully joined, held in place by only a weak lattice of sinew and muscle, and with each step, Able could feel them grind against each other.

But he climbed.

And climbed.

His pace slowed further, each step a decision he had to make and from which he had to rest. Before long he noticed the shadows had lengthened before him, and the sunlight had slipped down his back. He hadn't considered spending the night on the mountain, but it looked as though he would have to.

He made a bed for himself in the gloaming, scraping together a pile of dried pine needles, and he lay there listening to the wind. His parents would no doubt be wondering where he had gone. They would have asked in the village. No one, not even his parents, would think he had gone up the mountain.

An owl screeched nearby, sounding lonely. Able wished it

well and fell into a heavy sleep from which only his throbbing hip could rouse him the next morning.

He was up before the sun, and held his breath against the pain as he struggled to his feet. It did not seem fair to him that something as small as his leg, something that had amounted to so little, could so overwhelm his body and mind. But he grabbed up his crutch and turned uphill.

The pain ebbed a bit as he loosened up, and in its place came thirst and hunger. He had been foolish not to bring water and food. But what was that against the foolishness in attempting the climb at all?

He was high enough now that the cool morning soon wrapped him in a fine mist that crept between the trees, clinging to the branches in tiny droplets. Able sucked the dew from the bitter, dusty pine needles until the rising sun finally reached over the mountain peak above him and burned the mist away.

In that dawn light, from around a tree, he spied a solitary hart standing on the mountainside but a stone's throw away. Able froze, downwind of the animal, and counted ten points on its branching antlers. He didn't know such beasts still roamed this forest, and had he the means, he would have reluctantly taken it. Instead he admired it, until his leg betrayed him and he stumbled.

The hart jolted at the noise, and in an instant had bounded off into the trees.

Able chose to take its appearance as a good omen, in spite of the dread he felt at what still lay ahead, and struggled on.

About midday, he came to the place that had defeated so

many who had come this way before, the place where the forest broke like a wave against a granite wall. Here the mountain shot upward, a nearly vertical face of craggy stone that stared down on the country below in cold indifference.

The wind had turned fierce, kicking dust from the ground and swiping grit from the cliff. Able looked at his crutch, which his father had carved for him, and then tossed it away. Then he took hold of the mountain by the folds in its skin and climbed.

He scaled the first fifty feet or so without difficulty. His arms were strong, and by them he lifted his body, using his good leg as an occasional strut, while his other leg dangled. But the roughness of the rock soon wore against his hands, and his arms grew weaker by degrees. A hundred feet up, they quivered dangerously. He wedged himself into a narrow crook in the cliff to rest them, one shoulder and most of his back against the stone.

The cliff raced downward from him at a fatal pace. But from that dizzying vantage, he saw the tiny village below, then studied the brown quilt of farmland, tracing and counting the fences like embroidered seams until he came to his family's small patch.

His mum and da were no doubt beset with worry for him. From their farm, he would appear a mere speck or blemish on the mountain's face, but he hoped his parents had chanced to look upward at that same moment he looked down.

When he felt some strength had returned to his hands and arms, he resumed his climb. Another fifty feet, and then another precarious rest. The wind beat him and lashed at him, as if trying to scrub him from the mountain's cheek. His fingers bled from under their nails, and his palms from blisters that had long since burst. But up and up he climbed.

When next he felt his muscles giving out and needed rest, he couldn't find any purchase with his good leg. He fought off a sudden panic and hung there calmly by his hands, testing every inch of stone within reach of his foot, but slipped each time. He was stranded, too weak to continue, yet unable to rest, a spider climbing glass. Desperation grew until he had to try his bad foot, and he found a little toehold. But as soon as he gave that foot the least weight, all the torment of the previous day's exertion ripped through every malformed fiber of his leg.

Able cried out, and his left hand lost its grip.

The world pivoted, he swung, but maintained his grasp on the rock with his right hand, his life at his fingertips.

He closed his eyes, breathing deeply for a few moments, and then assessed his hanging position. He realized he could now reach that toehold with his left foot, and upon doing so he was able to take some of the strain off his arm.

A falcon screeched in the sky as it launched from the cliff above, and Able watched it circle overhead. He could imagine the bird's confusion at the frail, ridiculous, awkward boy clinging to its aerie. Eventually, it shot skyward and vanished.

After resting a few minutes more, he heaved himself upward, grinding his jaw. He thought of home. His da's stubborn refusal to replace that old axe handle. His mum's warbling singing voice.

And he climbed on.

Until his hand reached up into nothing, because there was no more mountain, and he hauled himself onto the promontory's ledge. There he lay, on his back, staring at the blue sky and the searing sun, his body shaking uncontrollably, his teeth chattering. Then the sky went dark, and it took a moment for Able to realize that someone stood over him, blocking the light.

He felt bony hands wedging themselves under his shoulders and arms, smelled the tang of onion and unwashed hair, and saw the upside-down face of a woman who looked as old as the mountain itself. Then he felt the ground slide underneath him and realized he was being dragged. Everything went dark with the sky, and when he awoke, he found himself in a bed that smelled faintly of dried urine.

The cottage around him seemed nearly derelict. Sunlight poked through holes in the thatch, and a gossamer shroud of cobwebs kissed the rafters. But a meager pile of embers glowed in the fireplace, and something sulfurous and vile simmered above them in a small kettle.

Able rubbed his head. Nothing but the mountain felt solid in his mind. He raised himself from the bed expecting soreness, but felt very little, and walked through the open door.

Outside, the cottage sat in the sun atop the mountain's pate, which was bald save for the gnarled and stubborn pine trees growing here and there among skids of gray stone. Away from the house, Able spotted a cairn, the stones of which had not yet settled.

"You!" An old woman canted toward him through a neglected vegetable patch. "You," she said, her voice the frantic sound of a hinge that had rusted shut. "You are here."

He was here, and here, it seemed, was the witch.

"The branch," she said.

Able did not know what that meant.

She shook her head, white hair a tangle, and then shook her hands. "The branch is weak, and the ants have got into it."

His unease grew. It seemed she expected him to respond, but he had no idea what to say. And something else felt different about himself.

She rapped her fingertips hard against her forehead, eyes squeezed shut, obviously frustrated. Then she suddenly stabbed her finger toward the sky. "No music!" She stamped her bare, filthy foot against the ground. "Silence. Deep down."

So the witch was mad. The stories had not mentioned that. Able felt his hopes plummet, as if he had fallen from the cliff after all. He did not know how to deal with a madwoman.

A silent moment passed in which they seemed equally bewildered. The witch's wild gaze never settled, and at last she clucked and shooed him back toward the cottage. "To bed, to bed."

He let her guide him inside, over to the sour bedding, thinking he'd sooner taste from her foul kettle than close his eyes in this place. But as she tucked him in, she crooned and said, "Thick grows the branch," and he found he could not keep his eyes open.

He did not know how long he slept, but it was night when

the witch tapped him awake. Shadows filled the cottage to the brim, and Able shot upright in bed.

She sat on the covers near his feet, hands in her lap, facing the fireplace's glow. "You're from the village, aren't you? I'd forgotten it. I forget a lot of things, these days, and then I remember them, and then I forget them again." She turned toward him, her face a fissured mask in the firelight. "Why've you come? Who are you?"

"I am Able," he said.

"That . . . is a good answer." She nodded as if she'd suddenly made up her mind about something. "There's a flute on the windowsill. I used to play it, back when I could hear the music. Perhaps you are the one to hear the music now. There's . . . a silence in me. Deep down in my bones. Ever since my husband . . ."

Able remembered the freshly piled cairn outside.

"I don't know where he's gone," she said. "I look for him, and sometimes I even believe I see him in the falcon, and the hart, and the owl. I shall not rest until I remember him again." She went quiet for some time, and then rose from the bed. "Your leg is mended. A sturdy branch for you. Now back to sleep."

Once more, Able's eyelids closed against his will, and when the morning woke him, he saw the embers in the fireplace had turned cold, and he knew the witch was gone. He rose from the bed and crossed to the narrow windowsill, where he found the flute.

It was a simple instrument, carved from a bone so ancient

it had turned to stone, the creature from which it had come turned to myth. Able took it outside into the sun, and only then did he notice he had walked there without limping. He looked down, and through the tattered remains of his trousers he saw a strong, healthy leg. An able leg.

But that was not why he had come. The drought still lay heavy on the land. He had failed, and the witch was gone.

He thought of his mum and da, of the life and love they had given him, how he wished he could have saved them, and by that thought, a gentle instinct brought the flute up to his lips. He took a breath and played a single note, resonant with untold years, and with it, the wind turned cool and damp.

He played another note, and another, letting his fingers move the way the flute seemed to want them to, hearing the flute sing back to him the music he heard inside. The sky darkened in a way the land had not seen for months and months. With each note, clouds gathered and multiplied, rolling in like great millstones, grinding out thunder and lightning. They spiraled around the mountain peak and Able churned them on. When the clouds let loose their rain on the mountainside, and the pastures, and the fields below, he wept.

The witch had gone, but Able heard the music now, and he would stay here at the top of the world to play it. He would send it raining down. His mum and da would stand by their green fields, and perhaps when they looked up and listened to the thunder and the wind, they would hear it, too.

Perhaps they would even hear his name.

BASEBALL

Baseball. It's the only thing I've ever loved as long as I have loved my parents and siblings. The word itself is like family to me.

When I was a toddler, perhaps shortly after learning to walk, my best friend was a big red plastic bat that was twice my size. I was a preacher's kid, and I'd walk around the annual church pig roast swinging the bat at anything that showed up in my tiny strike zone. A fence post. A horsefly. A human leg. Another toddler. Can you imagine? The preacher's kid milling about with a giant red bat, bashing old ladies' legs and whacking little kids in the face? It's a wonder my parents didn't put me on the rotisserie with the pig.

My most memorable baseball day happened when I was ten. That year, I made the all-star team in my Little League. Our team traveled to small towns around Indianapolis, playing in tournaments and battling other all-star teams for local pride.

Our coach was all business. He wore a black whistle around his neck. During practice, he belted ground balls through the dirt

177

and made us field them barehanded. If we weren't playing to our potential, he made us run laps, and then he belted more ground balls at us. To say the least, we were prepared for tough situations.

One tournament brought us to Rushville, a tiny town located southeast of Indianapolis. The first day of the tournament we won one game and lost one, putting us in the losers' bracket. One more loss and we'd be going home. We had to keep winning if we wanted to stay and play.

On Sunday, the last day of the tournament, we played our first game at eight o'clock in the morning. From eight until noon we won three games in a row, which earned us a spot in the championship game that same evening. We were on a hot streak. But it was a typical Indiana summer, full of heat and humidity, and we were physically and emotionally drained.

During the championship game, we were down three runs in the early innings. We had fought our way to the title game, but in our dugout there was little hope of defeating a well-rested, high-caliber team.

It was the bottom of the third inning. I was playing shortstop. I clearly remember what happened next, because I've replayed the moment a thousand times in my head.

The batter hit a pop-up down the first-base line, in foul territory. Our first baseman—his name was BJ—turned and ran, holding his glove in the air. He caught the ball and slammed against the chain-link fence. The crowd erupted; even the opposing team's parents cheered. It was a tremendous backhanded catch, especially for a ten-year-old.

But when BJ returned to his position at first base, his face was bright red and he couldn't catch his breath. He leaned over, hands on his knees, trying to take in as much air as he could. But he couldn't breathe.

BJ took out his asthma inhaler and took two puffs from it. He lay down on the dirt, panting harder, his chest rising and falling in sudden bursts. Our coaches rushed out of the dugout, and then BJ's parents hurried down from the bleachers. More parents brought over cold towels and placed them on BJ's forehead and arms. Then sirens echoed through the park. The ambulance sped through the lot and stopped next to the same chain-link fence where BJ had made the spectacular catch.

I stood, silent, with my teammates just behind the pitcher's mound. I'd seen kids twist an ankle or fall awkwardly on a wrist, but I'd never seen someone who couldn't breathe. This was way more serious.

The paramedics lifted BJ onto a stretcher and wheeled him toward the ambulance. BJ's face was as pink as bubble gum and covered with an oxygen mask. He was panting harder than before, and his eyes, his terrified eyes, were filled with fear.

BJ was my teammate and friend. We had played on the same team in the regular season, and now I didn't know if he'd be okay or not. The last thing I wanted to do was play more baseball. I wanted to give him my next breath of fresh air.

Sirens wailed, and the ambulance sped away. Our coach gathered our entire team on the pitcher's mound. He told us that BJ would be okay, and then instructed us to focus on the game, because that's what BJ would want us to do. No one spoke, but we all nodded.

In the last inning, we were losing by two runs and down to our final out. But we kept fighting. We strung together one hit after another, and loaded the bases. The hits kept coming, and we won the game!

After the celebration and trophy presentation, we visited the local hospital. There was BJ, breathing like his old self and smiling at his new championship trophy.

Baseball.

It provides moments of tragedy and triumph, and tests the very depths of the human spirit. Like I said, the word itself is like family to me.

POP!

The truth was, my arm was killing me.

I spit out the last of my sunflower seeds through the chain-link fence, and straightened the bill of my hat. I adjusted my belt, making sure the silver clasp was in the middle, right above my zipper. I turned to the bench and, while avoiding my bustling teammates, picked up my glove. Then I walked out of the dugout and headed toward the pitcher's mound. On my way, I hopped over the white chalk that made up the third baseline.

Coach Taylor's dad was superstitious. He always sat in the first row. He always wore the same Cincinnati Reds hat. And he always told me . . .

Never step on the chalk. Never. No matter what. It's bad luck.

Raymond, our shortstop and best player, ran up and rested his hand on my back, probably right between the one and zero on my jersey. "Three outs, Brett, just three more outs," he said.

I nodded.

Raymond jogged to his position between second and third

base, and began fielding ground balls from Lucas, our first baseman.

In only seven words, our best player had put the game on my left arm. Three more outs and we were city champs. Just three more outs. But I'd pitched all season, and I'd already pitched a complete game in the city tournament. The pain in my arm started in my left shoulder and burned all the way to the inside part of my elbow. But I kept it inside, hidden, locked away. My team needed me.

I bent over and, with my bare hand, snatched the Rawlings baseball off the infield grass. I tucked my glove under my arm and massaged the ball in my hands. The ball didn't feel right. It felt slippery, like it would sail from my fingertips and land halfway up the backstop.

I held the baseball up to the umpire. When he looked at me, I tossed the ball to him, and he caught it using his umpire's mask. He reached in the black bag resting on his hip, pulled out a brand-new baseball, and tossed it to me. I took it from my glove and looked it over. It was too white, too easy for the batter to see. The sun had just set behind the forest beyond the right field fence, and I didn't want the batter locking in on a bright white meteor coming down the pipe. But I also didn't want to annoy the umpire by asking for another ball.

Instead, I bent down next to the pitching rubber and picked up a handful of dirt. With my glove tucked securely under my right arm, I added a little spit and rubbed the dirt into the bright white leather of the ball. While rubbing up the new ball,

I strolled behind the pitcher's mound, waiting for Jackson, my catcher, to strap on his shin guards and chest protector. There, hanging over the center field fence, loomed the electronic scoreboard's yellow lights.

Home — 1.

Visitor — 0.

We were the home team. But everyone knew we shouldn't have made it to this game. No one would've predicted us to be winning, that's for sure.

Heading into the City Championship, we had lost three out of our last four games. Even worse, before the city tournament began Coach Taylor took a leave of absence because his dad got really sick. His dad loved watching our games. He'd sit in the first row of the bleachers — probably because his fragile bones couldn't handle walking any farther — his big glasses tucked underneath the bill of his Cincinnati Reds hat.

But now Coach Taylor's dad was gone forever, and Coach Taylor was back in the dugout.

"Come on, Brett! Just you and Jackie!" Coach Taylor shouted, clapping twice.

Jackie is what he calls Jackson, who was now crouched behind home plate, waiting for me to begin my warm-up pitches.

But my arm couldn't handle any more warm-up pitches. Every time I threw the ball, it felt like a thousand tiny needles were trying to escape from my shoulder.

There's a difference between soreness and pain. This was

pain. A sharp, piercing pain that got worse with each pitch. In the first inning, I was fine. Second and third inning, still fine. The pain showed up in the fourth inning, and ever since then I'd kept it locked inside of me, hoping it would disappear, hoping it would break up and dissolve into my bloodstream and never come back. But the pain stayed, and with each pitch it was getting worse.

All we needed were three more outs, and then there'd be no more pain. I could rest all summer, let my muscles and tendons and bones, or whatever was hurting so badly, heal for months. I couldn't let my team down now. They needed me. We had other arms that could pitch, but those kids weren't pitchers, they were throwers. Our real pitchers had already spent their innings for the week. I had all seven innings left. It was all on me. On my left arm. One more inning, just one more. Three more outs.

I stood on the pitching rubber, staring into Jackson's glove. The bleachers around home plate were packed. More people leaned over the fences down both foul lines. This was the last game of the season for everyone, and here I was, standing on the hill above it all, with a chance to win the championship. Only one team wins its last game of the season, and that team could be us.

I stepped back, wound up, and threw my first warm-up pitch. As the ball flew out of my hand, a fire ignited in my shoulder. It spread to my elbow, and stayed there, pulsating and breathing like a wild flame searching for more oxygen. I bent over, keeping the fire inside, locking it away, hiding it from the batter standing in the on-deck circle.

I waved Jackson to the pitcher's mound. He stood from his crouched position and jogged toward me. With our backs to home plate, we walked up the dirt incline.

"What's wrong, man?" Jackson said through his catcher's mask.

"My arm," I said. "No more warm-ups."

Jackson stared at me through the two horizontal bars of his catcher's mask. He looked down at my elbow. "Three more outs," he said. "You can do it."

Jackson jogged back to home plate. He said something to the umpire, and then the umpire looked at me.

Never step on the chalk. Never.

The first batter walked to the plate. He was the leadoff hitter. He was short and fast, probably the fastest player between both teams. He dug his back foot into the dirt and touched home plate with his bat.

I stared in at Jackson. From his crouched position, he flashed his index finger, the sign for a fastball. I nodded and began my windup. The ball flew from my hand, and the internal flames leaped from my shoulder to elbow. I clenched my teeth, holding the fire inside.

The batter swung, and the ball rolled softly between first and second base. I ran toward the first base side and up the baseline to cover the bag. Lucas fielded the ball and flipped it underhand to me. I caught the ball and touched first base with my right foot.

"Out!" shouted the umpire.

Cheers from the crowd.

"That's it, Brett!" Raymond said, standing near second base. "Come on, now! Two more outs!"

With the ball in my glove, I walked to the pitcher's mound. I glanced back at the first baseline. There was my footprint. On the chalk.

Never step on the chalk. Never. It's bad luck.

But it happened during a play, when I was hustling to cover first base, not when I was walking to the pitcher's mound. That should make it okay.

I reached down for another handful of dirt. The intense pain came when I threw the ball, but the dull ache in my shoulder wouldn't go away, either. I rubbed up the ball, looking at Jackson for the sign. Fastball. Curveball. Changeup. It was his choice.

The second batter smoothed the dirt in the batter's box with his cleats. He gripped the bat and took his stance.

Jackson flashed two fingers. He wanted a curveball.

I wound up, and the ball spun end over end from my fingertips. My shoulder and elbow roared with life, but the ball went where it was supposed to go.

The batter swung. The ball flew straight up into the twilight sky, above the infield.

Raymond called everyone off. "Mine, mine, mine!" he shouted. He camped underneath the ball and let it fall into his glove.

Two outs.

The crowd cheered.

I kept the fire down, locked inside my left arm.

"Come on, Brett!" Coach Taylor said. "One more out!" He clapped three times, pacing in the dugout. The rest of our team was hanging on to the dugout fence. They were ready to celebrate, ready to jump in a pile on the pitcher's mound.

The crowd stood.

Jackson called time to the umpire, and jogged to the pitcher's mound. He looked at me, breathing hard. "You okay?" he said.

I looked down at the baseball in my hand. The white leather was now a dirt-stained cover. The red stitches blazed a trail around the ball.

"One more out," he said. "Then you can rest."

I took the baseball and pounded it in my glove.

Jackson jogged back toward the batter and umpire, and crouched behind home plate.

The batter was number nine. For some reason, every team had a number nine. And he was always the best hitter. This team was no different.

Number Nine smoothed the dirt and dug in. He squatted down low, ready to explode on the next pitch near the strike zone. While staring at me, he spit on the plate.

Jackson flashed one finger. Fastball.

I took a deep breath, trying to release the inferno in my shoulder. I lay two fingers across the seams of the baseball inside my glove. I stepped back, wound up, kicked high, and let the ball go.

Number Nine swung and missed.

I adjusted my belt, feeling for the metal clasp. I grimaced while straightening the bill of my hat. The pain was rearing its head, trying to escape. It took all of my energy to keep it locked inside.

Number Nine adjusted his helmet and dug in. He spit again.

Jackson put three fingers down. Changeup.

I gripped the baseball like holding an egg, wound up, and reared back to throw the pitch.

When I let go of the ball, my shoulder popped, as if it were starting to come unhinged at the joint.

Number Nine swung, and it sounded like a sledgehammer hitting a flagpole.

The baseball rocketed off his bat, sailing high and far down the third base line. It cleared the outfield fence, and disappeared into the darkening sky.

"Foul ball!" shouted the home plate umpire, his hands in the air.

The crowd groaned with disapproval.

But Number Nine didn't think twice about it. He knew it was foul. He picked up his bat and gripped it tightly in front of his face.

The umpire threw me a new baseball. I leaned down and gathered a handful of dirt and rubbed it into the leather cover. I put the ball in my glove and gripped the seams with two fingers. I wanted to throw a fastball, though my shoulder and elbow begged me not to.

I stood on top of the pitcher's mound, waiting for the sign.

Jackson flashed one finger.

"Come on, Brett!" Coach Taylor yelled from the dugout.

I took a deep breath and let my shoulders down, trying to relax, but the pain in my left arm made my hand shake.

Number Nine took his stance and glared at me.

Jackson put his glove out, steadying the target.

I gripped the baseball, my hand trembling.

I wound up, reached back, and let it fly . . .

POP!

. . . I grabbed my shoulder . . .

. . . Number Nine swung the bat . . .

. . . I collapsed on the dirt . . .

. . . buried underneath my teammates . . .

Jane Yolen

WHAT REALLY HAPPENED

THE HOME MAKER

The summer I was thirteen and off to camp in Vermont with my younger brother, escaping the heat of a New York City apartment, I got a peculiar letter from my mother. She informed me that we would be picked up by our Aunt Iz and Uncle Harry and brought to our new home in Connecticut.

New home?

We'd had no warning. That meant no good-byes to our city friends, no choosing what to pack and bring, no picking out curtains and bedspreads, wallpaper, and all the stuff that goes into a teenager's room.

The whole of the new house—a ranch on an acre of prime land in Westport, the town Martha Stewart would call home thirty years later—had already been decorated by Harry and Iz. As they were interior decorators and quite sought after, it was a great honor.

We rode to our new home where my brother and I both had bedrooms half the size of the ones we'd had in New York. Mine was decorated for Harry and Iz's idea of who I *should* be, not who I was. I was horse mad, a ballet freak who loved folk music and reading, and wrote poetry. I dressed in dark shades, had cropped hair. The room boasted plaid wallpaper and a matching coverlet. The curtains were shades of teal and pink. There was no bookcase and no room for my record player. The loss I felt was incalculable. Maybe I wasn't an interior decorator, but I wanted it to be *my* room, and somehow it never was. I spent my high-school years there and never felt as if it was mine.

No, I didn't say this to my parents because they were so proud of the new house and its furnishings. And I never told Iz and Harry because they were my favorite aunt and uncle. Until writing this, I'd never spoken about it in print. But in that long ago incident, like an irritation under the skin that never quite goes away, the one thing that always stuck with me is that it's not the *house* that makes a home—it's the people inside who do.

MOVING HOME

have no stories of family drama in my childhood. My parents were hippies and we lived with a barn-full of artisans who created the most amazing silver, leather, and pottery items. My younger brothers and I had fields to explore and a pool tucked behind one of the barns. We had our own pottery wheels and the potters baked our pots in the kiln with theirs. My mom was a writer and my dad a professor who loved birds. I grew up and moved away.

My family was different. Not bad, but different. My children are twelve years apart, and we lived in Myrtle Beach, South Carolina, on a cul-de-sac next to our best friends, the Napiers.

Everything was just fine until crisis struck. Back at home, my dad was diagnosed with cancer. Suddenly, there was too much distance between my family and my parents.

I called my brothers—both equally far away. Someone needed to go home. I wanted it to be me. Both my brothers agreed that they were not able to pack up and relocate and loved the idea that I was willing—and ready—to do so. My husband agreed. Then we needed to talk to our daughters. They were reluctant, of course. They didn't want to leave their home.

So, as a family, we sat down to write a pros-and-cons list of moving. At first, the list was hard to figure out. I knew what my kids would gain by moving—their grandparents, full-time. Plus a hometown on a farm, surrounded by family and art and education. But my kids were dubious. All they could add to the list weighted the con side.

For a week, we worked on that list. As the days went by, the cons all got crossed out, replaced by counterparts on the pro side. Changing schools, for example, had originally begun as a con, but as we talked it out, it started to look like an adventure. Pro. Leaving the beach, which we would miss, but rarely went to anyway, got turned into mountains and changing seasons. Pro, pro. In the end, nothing on the con side survived except leaving the Napiers. But Nana and Papa outweighed everything else.

As we packed up and moved—my youngest and me first, then my elder daughter, then my husband with all our belongings in a big truck, we knew that it was family that was bringing us home, and the decision was right because we had made it as a family. No stories, especially true ones, have perfect happily-ever-afters. Though this story ends well, we do still miss the Napiers.

Jane Yolen and Heidi E. Y. Stemple

THE STORY

THE MARTHA STEWART BLUES

Who needs a fairy godmother when we've got Martha Stewart?" Mama always said. And she meant it, too. Every time she watched that program or bought the magazines, we had some kind of a home improvement project or a makeover — like some fancy new dish for dinner or a new organization for the bathroom or a newly fenced-in garden of exotic bulbs.

In elementary school she was known as the Martha Stewart Mom, because she always brought in special treats for the kids, for the teachers, or for the principal, Mr. Galveston, wrapped in colored papers and tied with ribbons in contrasting colors. When I hit high school she just brought in holiday treats for the teachers' room.

But there were times, the rough times, when she took makeovers much too far.

When Grandpa Dan died, Mama cut everyone's hair. She sheared her own off first to show us how to be brave. It had been long enough for her to sit on, but she took her big meat cutters and lopped off the single big braid in one loud snip. Tied the braid off top and bottom and put it away in a dresser drawer. Next she gave Grandma a severe bob, so different from her usual lazy blue waves. Then she tackled my hair, layering it so fiercely, I ended up with a kind of ocean effect all across my head. Then she gave Max a crew cut so he looked like a marine on hard duty. And finally she cut off every bit of baby Daniel's curls.

When Grandma died, Mama took her cue from the sound of our preacher hollering about "We all have to *die* some time!" The big turkey wattle under his throat, which usually made me want to giggle every time it vibrated, only made me sadder. I turned to Mama for comfort, but she was staring straight ahead, with that look in her eye as if she'd seen the Light. Soon as we got home, she said one word, really loudly.

"Die!"

Then she dyed all our hair. Mine came out a bright red. I was the lucky one.

And when Daddy moved out, with a girlfriend none of us had even suspected he had—though we *should* have, with him staying late at the office every single night and the weekends, too—Mama painted every room in the house. Painted over the wallpaper and the chipboard, with a color called Peony Orange with great stripes of Nasturtium Pink. All except the bathroom, which she painted Araucana Teal. From the Martha Stewart collection, of course.

★ ★ ★

It was only when Martha Stewart got convicted for making over the truth—lying to the police about insider stock trading—that Mama cried. She cried so much, we thought she was going to die of it. She stayed in her bedroom for three solid days—the weekend and the Monday that followed—and it didn't look as if she was going to come out any time soon.

"Boys," I said to Max and Daniel, who were four and five years younger than me, "we have to do something." My voice was low and serious, so they knew I meant it.

Daniel's face screwed up into what Mom always called his monkey look. "But what?"

Shrugging, Max said coolly, "Call the police? Call the doctor?"

"I'd sooner call Daddy," I said, which shut him up.

So we sat staring at each other—the TV off—the only sound that of the bird clock hooting the hours, reminding us that time was passing.

"I know," I said when the bird clock finished its four o'clock hoot. "We'll make her into the Ultimate Martha Stewart Mom. She'll like that. She'll be bigger than Martha Stewart."

Daniel's monkey face relaxed.

Max grinned. "And not in jail, either."

★ ★ ★

So that very afternoon we tried baking chocolate cookies, using Mom's well-underlined and cooking-oil-smeared Martha Stewart cookbook. I organized us into a team. The oven was my bailiwick, since Daniel was still too young to fool with hot things. But he was a superhero with the hand mixer. And Max liked measuring since it meant using math.

It took us far longer than Martha Stewart said. And the first batch was burned. But we didn't give up. We were doing this for our mom.

Mom didn't appreciate the cookies, pushing them around the plate with a stiff finger. She ignored the flour that was coating the entire kitchen like a floury sandbox, courtesy of Daniel. Even when he went running in to her room to beg for forgiveness for making the mess, she ignored him and kept crying.

★ ★ ★

The second day we stayed home from school and I called in, my voice deep as Mom's, saying we all had the flu. I had written down everything I planned to say and read it carefully off the sheet of paper.

"You do sound bad, Mrs. Callan," the school secretary said. "I hardly recognize your voice."

"That's because . . . ," I began, knowing that ad-libbing was a bad idea, ". . . I have a sore, sore throat."

Behind me Max exploded into laughter that transmogrified into a throaty cough.

I hung up without further explanation.

"I don't think you sound like Mom at all," whispered Daniel.

"Mom with a bad throat," I said.

"Not even that." He looked at me funny.

"Well, we don't have to fool you," Max said, "only the school."

I nodded. "And thank goodness for that."

We'd decided to clean the house—flour and all—and we knew we'd never be able to do it with the little time after school, which was why we had stayed home. I hated telling lies, but I hated Mom's crying even worse. So when she was off at work and we were home from school, that was our only opportunity.

We started in the kitchen, Max on vacuum, Daniel on feather duster, and me with the rubber gloves and chemicals, 'cause I'm the oldest.

We were doing well, too, until we threw the good teal towels into the washer along with the bleach. Well, Max threw in the towels, and I threw in the bleach. The teal towels were now pale spotty aqua. Who knew? Mom had never let us near the stuff before.

When the spotted towels didn't faze her one bit, and she just turned her head to the wall and kept on her Martha Stewart–crying, we figured it was time for more drastic measures.

★ ★ ★

Day three brought the official Mama Makeover. I called the school again and said, "All my kids are really sick and me, too." And there was enough flu around so no one questioned it. Or so I thought. And I wasn't lying all that much, as Mom was home sick from work. And crying.

I got out Mom's makeup kit and brought it to her bed. Daniel painted her toenails a lovely shade of pink. Max did her fingernails a shimmery blue. He refused to touch the pink—it simply wasn't manly enough. Boys are weird.

I tackled her face.

We were way beyond Martha Stewart now. More like Mardi Gras by way of Bozo the Clown. Unfortunately, even the paint-outside-the-lines toes, the manly fingers, and the Bozo eye shadow didn't lift Mom's spirits. It didn't even get her off the bed and out of her room. She just wept off most of the makeup, even though it said on the bottle that it was water-resistant. She had runnels and runoffs going all down her face.

We'd been screening all our calls on the caller ID, and each time the school phoned, we didn't answer. I had carefully written out the number so neither of the boys would even lift the receiver.

But then Dad called, and Daniel knew that number and picked up the phone and shouted, "Dad! We're all sick!"

I grabbed the phone and said, "Just the flu. Nothing to worry about."

"I can come over, sweetie," he said. "Tiffany can help."

Tiffany. She was hardly old enough to vote, much less be Dad's girlfriend. We didn't want her to try to fix anything, and maybe later laugh about Mom with Dad.

So I told Dad—okay, I lied to Dad—that everyone was fine, especially Mom when she wandered out into the kitchen in her bathrobe and the now-smudged and runny makeover makeup from yesterday still on her face.

"Mom?" I said.

Dad said, "Let me talk to her."

The boys were eating the breakfast I had made them of

Cheerios with slices of banana, and the little kitchen TV was on CNN because no one had thought to turn on cartoons yet. A pretty blonde was talking, but the three of us had not been listening.

Mom was.

It was already too late when I heard what the blond reporter was saying. It must have been a slow news day because they were actually running a segment on living in a women's prison entitled "What will it be like if Martha goes to jail?"

Mom was staring at the TV and making strange sounds, more like an animal in pain than a person.

Dad shouted in the phone, "Lizbeth? What is it? What is it?"

And I said, "Cat. Caught in door. Gotta go." And I hung up, hoping like mad that he believed me. Hoping he didn't remember that Daniel is allergic to ragweed, flatfish, pine, and animal dander, and that we had no cats.

It was panic time. I looked at Max and Max looked at Daniel and Daniel looked at me.

"What do we do?" Daniel whispered in his little-boy voice.

Max grabbed my hand, something he hadn't done since he was old enough to cross a street by himself.

And I said, almost without thinking, "Un-makeover." And then I realized I was brilliant and right and told them quickly what we needed to do.

First we would have to unmake Mom, literally and figuratively.

"Daniel—you're in charge of water," I shouted.

He looked at me, monkey-faced again.

"Mom's shower!" I told him.

He ran down the hall to her bathroom and turned it on.

Max needed no such telling. He took Mom by the arm and dragged her out of the kitchen and into the bathroom.

I, being the only girl, undressed her and then sat her on the toilet and, with some old lotion I found in the cupboard, cleaned away her smudged clown makeup. Then I shoved her into the shower.

She went in without complaint.

Meanwhile, the boys were in the kitchen and the living room erasing all traces of Martha Stewart—magazines, books, our pictures hung on big grosgrain ribbons, the pinecone turkey Thanksgiving place markers, the fancy spouted green bottle Mom kept the dish soap in. All gone.

It was a huge job. The house looked strange and bare.

After I put Mom back in bed, in a clean bathrobe and no makeup, we took turns sitting with her, reading her our homework—my report on the Incas, Max's book report about *The Lion, the Witch and the Wardrobe,* and Daniel's "I Can Read" books.

Then we took another turn: my violin practice, Max's math facts, Daniel's counting. She didn't complain, but she didn't show the kind of joy she usually did during what she always said was her favorite part of the day.

Whoever was not sharing with Mom was on "Eradicate Martha Stewart Duty." We unhung the good linens and stuck them in drawers the way normal people did. We took the ribbons off the kitchen bulletin board. We threw out *all* the throw pillows.

When we finally dragged Mom out of her room late that afternoon, into the main part of the house, it didn't look great. But it didn't look Martha Stewart, either.

"This is not a good thing," Mom said, taking a deep breath and looking all around. But at least she was talking.

Then she walked from room to room with the three of us trailing behind her like a line of ants, afraid to stray from the path lest we become lost and never find the group.

We probably all looked pretty pathetic. But we didn't care. At least Mom was no longer crying. Her eyes were still red from days of it, and big from the shock of the newly unmade house. But she didn't shed another tear.

★ ★ ★

Our parade ended in the bathroom, which looked the most pitiful of all. We had attempted to strip the painted-over wallpaper by running a very hot shower to steam it loose. But we'd only succeeded in pulling great jagged strips from the wall. Gone were the homemade soap and stainless steel cotton swab holders. There was not a fabric-lined basket in sight.

We piled in after Mom. In the still-foggy oversized vanity mirror, four tense and pasty faces stared back at us.

We waited a minute. Two. I saw Daniel trying hard to keep from making the monkey face. Three. Max actually stood still as the wall—something I didn't think he was capable of.

Four. I swear I held my breath till I nearly turned blue. Five.

And then something broke the silence. The doorbell.

"Dad?" I mouthed, and the mirror image told us all.

"Dad!" we all said.

Mom threw her head back and raised her hands to her face. Her shoulders shook and we all looked at one another, slumped and dejected. I had run out of ideas.

A sound escaped through Mom's hands.

More sobs? I thought. *Please, no more sobs.*

But, it was not. What echoed in that crowded, torn-up bathroom was not crying, but laughter.

We all threw our arms in one great big circle around Mom and laughed with her.

And that was how our parade sidestepped and stumbled to the door—in one big soggy-from-the-steamy-bathroom, dirty-from-the-eradication-campaign, red-eyed, hysterically-laughing, Martha Stewart–free ball of family. Mom was back. We were saved. Nothing could possibly go wrong now.

★ ★ ★

As we had guessed, Dad was at the door. And Tiffany. And the principal, Mr. Galveston. Oh, and the UPS man, but he just took one look at all of us, dropped the package he was holding, and disappeared.

Everyone spoke at once.

"Joan, what is going on here? I know the kids are lying to me and won't let me talk to you. You'd better tell me what is happening." That from Dad.

"Mrs. Callan, I was told that your daughter was impersonating you on the phone, which is quite a serious offense. And, we have not been able to get anyone on the phone all day long." The principal.

"Where's that new kitty-witty? Oh, I just love baby animals!" Tiffany, of course.

In Mom's fragile state, I knew I was going to have to handle everything. What I had to come up with was a good story. I had just about come up with a whopper about a runaway cat and an allergy-induced, dander-borne illness that affected Mom's voice in some strange and purely temporary way, when Mom stepped in front of me.

"Stewart," she said to Dad, in that voice she uses especially for corralling wayward children. "I have told you to please call before you bring your *friend* here." When she said the word *friend,* her voice practically dripped of eye-rolling. "I will thank you to keep our agreements as stated in our divorce papers or I will have to take you back to court." This last part she said with a smile on her face in the airiest, lightest, most nonchalant voice. I was *so* impressed.

"Mr. Galveston," she continued, "so nice of you to come in person. I didn't know principals did that these days."

I squirmed. How was Mom going to lie her way out of this mess? The mess we kids had made trying to help her.

"As you all can see"—she swept a hand past the three of us, and *boy* did we look pitiful after our long day of tearing the house apart and doing our best to look physically ill (Daniel coughing, Max sniffling, and me not needing to pretend much since my stomach was really twisted into knots)—"the kids and I have had a rough day, but I am sure we will all rally in the morning."

With that, she dismissed the three of them with a regal wave of her hand and closed the door, but not before Daniel had scooted out to retrieve the UPS package.

★ ★ ★

That night we ate omelets for dinner—mine with spinach and feta cheese, the boys' with cheddar, and Mom's with hot sauce. And as we ate, I wondered what would happen next. We had unmade the house and tried to make over our mother from a Martha Stewart clone to the mom we thought she could, should, or wanted to be.

I helped with the dishes, Max tied up the garbage, Daniel flattened the eggshell carton for the recycle bin. But when I looked over at Mom sitting at the table drinking her tea, I realized that she had already performed her own makeover. She had done what Martha Stewart had not been able to. She had gotten herself and us out of trouble without ever telling a lie.

"Kids," she said, when we were done with our chores, "my amazing, wonderful kids, come here. We need to work together to make this a Wilber house, not a Martha Stewart–house. So it's up to you to tell us what to do. Not some lady far away in a magazine."

We gathered around the table and Daniel spoke first.

Screwing up his face, he blurted out, "I want a green bathroom with a frog and lizard border."

"Sounds cool," Mom said.

"Can we . . . ," Max said, ". . . just have a little less . . ."

"Pink?" Mom asked.

He nodded.

"You got it, my big boy. Maybe something more electric-colored!"

"Way cool . . . ," he said and grinned.

She turned toward me. Her eyes were shining. Not with tears this time, but with something very close to laughter. "And Lizzie?"

I couldn't say anything. Not for the longest time. Then I whispered, "I just want you, Mom. Not Martha Stewart. You. And I just want everyone to be happy."

"The hardest to manage of course," Mom said, reaching out a hand and grabbing mine. "But with everyone in the family's help, how can we fail?"

And the UPS package? That was the super-deluxe Martha Stewart Preserved Blue Hydrangea Wreath for the front door. Max gasped when he saw the invoice in Daniel's hand. Mom took it from him and laughed. "What do you think I should do with this, kids?"

But I knew at once. "Give it to Tiffany," I said. "A peace offering. Let *her* be the next Martha Stewart. We've got our mom."

Mike Winchell

WHY OR WHY NOT?

Asking Questions about the World Around You

I had an imaginary friend named Mork when I was four years old. He wasn't just my imaginary friend, though, since I also claimed he was my younger brother. My parents were welcoming of Mork for a while. They didn't act worried or tell me Mork wasn't real. Instead, sometimes they would ask about Mork, you know, just to see how he was doing. In time, Mork disappeared from my imagination, but his existence brings up a number of questions.

Question: Why did I create Mork in my mind?

Answer: I had two older brothers, so maybe I created Mork because I wanted a younger brother, too.

Question: What was with the name of this imaginary person? Why *Mork*?

Answer: At the time, there was a popular TV show called *Mork and Mindy*, and the main character was an alien named Mork who was living on Earth. Apparently, my young mind had decided my imaginary friend and brother should be named Mork.

Question: Why did Mork disappear from my imagination?

Answer: I don't know. This is still a mystery to me, but maybe it's because that's when I started making real friends and Mork wasn't needed anymore.

In the following stories, our authors answer questions about the world around them. Adam Rex decides whether or not an object can be a friend. Cuban author Margarita Engle considers how your ancestors factor in to your present-day family. Author Kate Messner looks at how aliens can be considered friends, enemies, or even family members.

Adam Rex

THE KNIGHT OF THE TRASH HEAP

When I was a kid, I found treasure all the time.

It helped that my standards were low. Besides, money was worth more in the seventies and eighties, so I felt pretty lucky just finding a penny. My bones are creakier now, so I won't bend over for less than a dime.

Once, my best friend found a diamond ring that was worth two hundred dollars. On the *ground*. That was all the reason I needed to scan gutters, check pay phones for forgotten coins, inspect all the neighbors' curbs on trash day.

I had just enough dignity not to lift an actual trash can lid and rummage through people's garbage like a raccoon, but I couldn't help casting my eyes toward a cardboard box that might also be sitting on the curb, awaiting pickup. So it was in one of these boxes that I saw him—a little knight in plastic armor, looking up from a bed of old magazines.

I glanced around for witnesses, because I was seven and just a little unsure about the dos and don'ts of stealing from other people's garbage. The coast was clear, so I snatched the knight and walked swiftly home while pretending to notice what a nice day it was.

In my bedroom I got a better look at him: gray plate armor with just a little hint of metallic jazz in the plastic; a blunt sword that snapped in and out of his cupped hand; a ring around his opposite arm where you could tell a shield was supposed to fit, but that was missing. Not the greatest-looking action figure, you understand—the sort of thing moms bought at the drugstore to get their kids to stop crying.

I didn't care—I had pretty flexible expectations back then, and for a few days the little knight filled in for the Darth Vader figure I'd loaned to a friend and never got back. The knight killed Obi-Wan; he sword-fought with Luke; he was secretly everyone's father, and when he told you so you screamed NOOOOOOOOOOOOOOOOOOOOOOOO! Luke's father, Chewie's father . . . everyone's father.

★ ★ ★

Eventually, Mom saw me playing with a toy she didn't recognize. She asked where it came from and I froze like it was my first lie. Twenty minutes later, I was still trying to explain the difference between a dry box of magazines and a wet can of smelly garbage as I watched Mom drop my knight into the cutlery basket of our dishwasher and turn it on.

Fine, I decided.

Fine.

He would probably come out of there looking *great*.

Shiny, like a real knight.

Dishwashers take a long time. I sat and waited, and I could feel steamy heat radiating out the avocado-colored door.

Finally Mom opened that door, and my knight looked... different. Mushy. A little like a birthday candle at the end of a party.

His sword had curled back into a self-defeating sort of U shape. In a cartoon he would have swung it at Bugs Bunny anyway and stabbed his own behind.

He wasn't Darth Vader–material anymore, anyway. Darth Vader didn't smell like lemon.

In 1980 you saw a film only as many times as you were willing to pay for it at the theater—only rich people and the president watched movies at home. I mention this to explain how it was that I decided my dishwashered knight looked *kind* of like an alien bounty hunter I barely remembered from a few seconds of *The Empire Strikes Back*.

I traded his U-shaped sword for a blaster and played with him dutifully, until I saw what an actual Bossk Bounty Hunter toy looked like. After that I unceremoniously buried my knight in the backyard.

We sold that house in 1990. I suppose he's still back there.

Rest in peace, faithful knight of the trash heap.

Recycling

by Adam Rex

Taking out the recycling is one of my jobs.

The bin is full of old, broken, used up things.

But there's still some good in them, and we can take what's good to make something new.

I like to check the neighbor's bins to see if there's anything worth saving.

Nope.

Nothing good in the Johnsons' bin, either.

The Tudors' bin has something interesting.

I bring it home.

This guy's all right.

While my knight is off bagging leaves, Buddy Houston walks by with his dog.

GOT A BOYFRIEND TO DO YOUR CHORES FOR YOU, HUH?

No.

SOMEDAY I'M GONNA HAVE A WIFE WHO CLEANS MY HOUSE AND GETS ME MY FOOD AND DOES WHATEVER I SAY.

Is this rapscallion bothering you, lady?

Ohboy.

Don't worry about it. Buddy's always teasing me. Mom says it's because he likes me.

DO NOT.

We watch Buddy and his dog run until we can't see them anymore.

But it *was* kind of funny.

Ideas can get old and broken, too.
   You take what's good in them and make something new,
                                 but you have to throw
                                 the rest away.

I told Mom and Dad that someone else did my chores, so I didn't
get my allowance that week. That's okay,
I didn't deserve it.

I never saw my
knight again.

I wonder what
happened to
him.

END.

INSPIRED BY CURIOSITY

When I was studying botany, I admired Alexander von Humboldt (1769–1859), a German nobleman who grew up in a castle and became a great explorer. He is often called the Father of Modern Geography, the First Ecologist, or my personal favorite: the Genius of Curiosity. All over the world, dozens of mountains, rivers, and ocean currents carry his name, because he was the first to map them. He was friends with Thomas Jefferson, and was admired by Charles Darwin. Ralph Waldo Emerson called von Humboldt one of the wonders of the world. Simón Bolívar described him as the true discoverer of the Americas.

So imagine my surprise when, during a visit to relatives in Cuba, my great-uncle told me that the Genius of Curiosity stayed in the home of a customs agent whose name can be seen on one branch of our huge, complicated family tree.

Over the years, many aspects of my books have grown from the pages of that family tree. I've learned about relatives who were farmers, poets, pirates, and patriots. I've learned that I carry a genetic marker for indigenous maternal ancestry, even though most history books still perpetuate the myth that all Cuban Indians are extinct. I've learned about strong women and men who defied tradition in various ways. Some of the family stories would have been forgotten, without that written family tree. Others are so deeply rooted in Cuban history that they would survive by oral storytelling, no matter how long ago the events occurred. The story of von Humboldt's visit is one of the tales that would keep being retold, simply because the Genius of Curiosity had an impact.

My great-uncle told me that von Humboldt referred to the women of Trinidad, Cuba, as charming and beautiful. He also mentioned a family joke about von Humboldt's visit, a joke that has been repeated for over two centuries: If *el sabio* (the wise man) was so educated, why was he always asking questions? Shouldn't he already have known all the answers? It was a joke that taught the importance of curiosity. I imagined how the children of many generations must have laughed at this simple joke, and then wondered about its meaning, because wise people do ask questions. Educated people remain curious. A spirit of wonder leads to learning.

It would be oversimplifying to assume that my present-day relatives love learning simply because they remember von Humboldt's visit. Nevertheless, some have become doctors, artists, and writers. From a humble farm background, many have gone on to study, travel, and explore. The Genius of Curiosity has been one of many influences, as has the fact that we learn because humans are wonder-filled, and that is because the natural world around us is wondrous.

After I returned to the United States, I read von Humboldt's diary, along with his essays about Cuba. Fascinated, I learned that even though he was chosen by the king of Spain to observe and map the geography, botany, and wildlife of the Spanish Empire, he noticed human nature, too. He took a bold stance against slavery, writing that his abolitionist views were the most urgent part of his studies. "To this very portion of my work," he claimed, "I attach greater importance than any experiments of magnetic intensity, or statistical statements." He also noted that he loved teaching the young, and found great satisfaction in helping curious children learn how to observe the natural world.

In the part of von Humboldt's diary that describes his overnight stay in Trinidad, Cuba, on March 14, 1801, I learned something about my own family history. Von Humboldt did not praise the beauty and charm of the women, as I had been told. Instead, he noted their "lively intelligence." Clearly, during the course of more than two hundred years of telling and retelling, our family legend had changed. Some modern historians believe that von Humboldt and his male assistant, Aimé Bonpland, were a couple, but in 1801, their relationship could not have been discussed openly. Perhaps my ancestors saw a way to make their honored guest more socially acceptable, by choosing to remember von Humboldt as a ladies' man.

All of this tells me that both history and science are constantly changing, as new facts are discovered, or old ones are viewed with a brighter light. So, in honor of the lively intelligence of girls and boys who love to learn, I have chosen to celebrate one of the world's most brilliant naturalists through the eyes of a diverse group of curious young people. I can't prove that children followed Alexander von Humboldt around my mother's hometown on March 14, 1801, yet I am certain that it must be true, because who wouldn't want to peek through a microscope and telescope? Would you?

REFERENCES

Von Humboldt, Alexander. *Ensayo Político Sobre la Isla de Cuba*. Introducción por Fernando Ortiz. Two volumes. La Habana: Talleres de Cultural, 1930.

Von Humboldt, Alexander. *Personal Narrative of a Journey to the Equinoctial Regions of the New Continent*. New York: Penguin Books, 1995.

Von Humboldt, Alexander. *The Island of Cuba*. Includes notes and a preliminary essay by J.S. Thrasher; an introduction by Luis Martínez-Fernández; "The Nature of Slavery," translated from German by Shelley L. Frisch; and Humboldt and Arango y Parreño, "A Dialogue," by Frank Argote-Freyre. Princeton, NJ: Markus Wiener Publishers, 2001.

Personal communication between the author and Julio Uría Peña. Unpublished family tree compiled by Manuel Moreno Fraginals.

THE GENIUS OF CURIOSITY

March 14, 1801
Trinidad, Cuba

On islands, storms bring surprises.
Messages in bottles, shipwrecked pirates,
creatures from the deep . . . and now, as if
to remind us of our isolation,
a famous scientist from far away
is blown ashore, like a leaf.

Baron Alexander von Humboldt
is a nobleman raised in a haunted castle.
That is all we know, beyond the way
grown-ups say he was chosen
by the King, to measure mountains,
map rivers, and gather feathers, bones,
and twigs from every strange bird, beast,

and spice
in the Empire.

Are there mermaids in his collection?
Unicorns, dragon's teeth, griffin wings?
We follow him everywhere he goes,
even though he does not act like a rich man
or a wise man. No! Instead he tramps around
in muddy boots, peering into dirty puddles
and gloomy caves. The things he collects
are quite dull. Sand, pebbles, insects,
and worms.

How long will you stay, we ask, because
we are eager to study his strangeness.
Until the wind shifts, he replies, giving
an answer that makes us feel as dull
as worms.

Does he prefer fancy cities? Are we boring?
Some of us are well dressed, but others
are raggedy. Some live in slave huts,
while others are free. Will he compare us
to the children of Alta California
and el Perú?

We need to learn about him quickly,
before he and his quiet assistant leave.
They have a microscope that makes
tiny mosquitoes look monstrous,
and a telescope that helps us believe
the moon is huge and dry like a desert,
with craters crisscrossed by scars.

We are confused.
If Alejandro *el sabio* is a genius,
then why does he constantly
ask questions? Shouldn't he already know
the names of hovering hummingbirds
and honey-scented flowers?

He asks us how long it would take
to hike to a place where we could help
measure the tallest trees, by using numbers
as if they were rulers. We laugh, but we
lead him, sharing our favorite
forest secrets, all the hidden
swimming ponds and parrot nests.

We notice that when the wise man
and his helper are together, they seem
like an old married couple, bickering
or laughing, so comfortable

with each other! All evening,
the two of them admire fireflies.

Then they vanish
into the comfortable home
of the customs agent.

In the morning, they are outdoors again,
asking us to show them how fishermen
catch sea turtles in the old way,
the ancient way, by tying a rope
to the tail of a suckerfish,
and waiting until the little fish
finds a big turtle, then attaches itself,
so that it can be used like a small boat
for towing a big ship.

The wise man shares his knowledge
of coral reefs, splashing into the water
as he explains how the orange stone
is not really a dead rock, but a living
colony of animals that resemble plants
with fluttering leaves and twisted
branches in rainbow colors,
like a mysterious undersea sky.

Later, in swamps, we watch
as the wise man is startled by the way
crocodiles chase daring horsemen.
Why do they ride so close, he demands,
but we know they just like the thrill.

Still, the way the wise man wonders
makes us wonder, too.

At a place where our river meets
the sea, we reveal legends about
manatee-*sirenas* who sing to enchant
lonely sailors, and we take turns
telling old stories about *los güijes,*
mischievous green trolls
that hide behind waterfalls,
and come out only to steal
chickens, or to tease weary wives
by moving laundry from one line
to another.

The wise man smiles at our tales.
He gathers our opinions, along with
his odd assortment of seashells,
seedpods, and iguana skins.

When he teaches us about fossils,
we show him a snail shell
made of stone.

He speaks of change, warning us that if
we grow up to be the greedy sort of farmer
who chops down trees to sell charcoal,
freshwater springs will dry up, and our climate
will change
forever.

Always ask questions, the wise man
advises. Don't just choose to believe
everything you've been told. You must
discover new ways to think, instead of
just memorizing the old thoughts
of old people.

Argue with unfairness, he adds,
gazing at those of us who are slaves.

So young, he mutters, shaking his head.
This will end, he promises, vowing to do
his own share of arguing with kings
back in Europe.

Europe.

Where is that?

So far!

Maps are his specialty.

He draws them on paper,

filling up notebooks

with swirly lines

and solid shapes.

We imitate his maps, scraping

islands and continents into our own

red mud.

Even though the wise man's short visit

has taught us so much about rivers, trees,

stones, and people, most of us agree

that the best thing we've learned

has no name. Is it kindness? Maybe.

We wonder about this, after we see

how the wise man argues with men

who kill baby pelicans

for no reason.

When the wise man shouts his protests,

the mean men don't care. They don't listen.

But we listen. We learn. Best of all,

we learn how

to learn.

Kate Messner

WHAT REALLY HAPPENED

DESERT DARKNESS

t is just after 4:00 a.m., but no one is sleeping. For one thing, the tents are too hot. The average summer temperature here in the Anza-Borrego Desert is 105 degrees, and today was hotter than average. But that's not the real reason we're staying up all night. This desert is home to a rare sight—one that's getting harder and harder to find on Earth. True darkness.

Late this afternoon, we bounced and jostled our way out here in old military jeeps. Joe, our guide from the desert tour company in the nearest town, taught us how to pitch tents in the sand and cooked up steaks and salmon on a grill. We hiked around for a bit, and he told us about the creatures that call this alien landscape home—the scorpions and snakes and stinkbugs. But the real show starts when the sun goes down and darkness falls over the rocks.

Tonight, there will be a total lunar eclipse. So instead of sleeping, we'll spend our hours of darkness sitting in camp chairs under the stars, watching a shadow creep over the moon. A lunar eclipse happens when a full moon passes through the

Earth's shadow. In the early stages just before 2:00 a.m. on this August night, it starts slowly and looks like someone has taken a tiny bite out of the moon.

As the moon continues into the darker part of the Earth's shadow, called the umbra, it turns a reddish, coppery color. That's because some indirect light still reaches the moon, even when it's in the Earth's shadow. That light has to pass through the Earth's atmosphere, though, where most of the blue light is filtered out, leaving the same reddish glow we sometimes see in the sky here on Earth at sunrise and sunset. Once the moon is dark, the next show begins.

"Come on up, you'll see the Orion Nebula." Our trip astronomer, Dennis Mammana, steps back from his telescope so I can take a look. "That's where stars are born."

Orion, the Andromeda Galaxy, and so many other celestial features are in full view. It has to do not only with the time—the night of the eclipse—but also with the place. The Anza-Borrego Desert is one of the darkest places in the United States, one of the few locations where city lights don't make it impossible to see the stars. That's why Mammana moved here from the East Coast. When he was a boy, he watched the stars from his home in Easton, Pennsylvania, between Philadelphia and New York City.

"I visit my hometown from time to time, and I don't know if I would have had the inspiration to study the sky with the light pollution that now exists," he says. "I used to be able to see the Milky Way from my backyard, but today I'm fortunate to see even the brightest stars from there."

Anza-Borrego, he says, is different. There are strict laws to control light pollution from city lights. Mammana is thankful for that and says he'll stay up all night anytime he has the chance to view a phenomenon like the total lunar eclipse.

Tonight, he clicks photographs from behind a second telescope. Coyotes howl from a distant ridge as the moon begins to emerge from the Earth's shadow. The stars begin to fade as the full moon lights up the desert sand once again.

"Watching such a celestial event gives one a true three-dimensional sense of the cosmos—here's the moon drifting through the sky and entering the shadow of our own planet. Seeing things like this and understanding that we can predict their occurrences gives people a recognition that the universe isn't 'out there,' but that we're *part* of the universe."

Part of it all, we sit in our camp chairs and stare up at the sky until the dark begins to fade. As the sun warms the sand, we crawl into our tents for a few hot hours of half-sleep.

In the morning, there are eggs and sausage cooked on a camp stove, coffee and orange juice sipped from tin cups. No one has slept enough, and by 9:00 a.m., with the temperature approaching 95 degrees, we are wilting in our folding chairs. Our guide, Joe, passes out squirt guns to the kids, and they have the most refreshing water war in the history of water wars. Even the sleepy grown-ups are happy to be targets in this heat.

"Squirt me!"

"Over here!"

As we begin to pack up for the bumpy ride back to our cars, one of the younger boys spots a stinkbug crawling under a rock.

"Gross!" he cries. He lifts the rock, then lifts his dusty sneaker to stomp. But Joe catches his arm. Not hard enough to hurt, but hard enough to throw him off balance. Hard enough that the bug can scuttle away into a shadowed crack in the earth.

"We don't do that out here," Joe says quietly. "This is his home—not yours."

The kid nods and cowers a little—Joe is not a small guy—and goes back to his squirt gun. My daughter, who loves bugs of all kinds, looks at me and gives a quiet nod. "Good for Joe," she says.

I agree. Joe and Dennis have given us all a gift on this sweltering desert weekend—shown us another kind of country, another landscape, and given us a glimpse of a world beyond our own. They've reminded us how vast and full of wonder the universe is. They've reminded us that we're not looking up at that universe—we're part of it, from a tiny armored insect in the desert sand to a new star being born light-years away.

Kate Messner

THEY MIGHT BE DANGEROUS

Whether or not there was intelligent life out there had never been a question. With half a trillion planets in the galaxy, millions of others must have had the right conditions for life. And everybody knew the aliens were coming. The electromagnetic signals had been increasing, so military watchers were on alert.

Alia and Zak had been taught to listen and watch for the telltale signs—screaming engine roars, bright flashes of light, and fireballs in the sky. But on the morning their mother sent them out to the market, there were none of those things.

All they heard was a muffled *whump* that sounded as if it had come from the far side of the recreation park. All they saw was a hint of a silver something, the way you might see an insect fly past in the corner of your vision, but by the time you turn to really look, it's flown off somewhere else.

Let's find out what it was! Alia veered from the well-traveled market path and took off, knowing her older brother would follow. She struggled to be still and attentive for lessons each day but loved racing through the desert on the way home, kicking up sand, skittering over rugged rocks on the far side of the park. She always pushed Zak to go beyond the boundaries their parents allowed. What was out there?

I don't see anything. Zak scuttled along the rocks with Mip panting at his side. He reached down to scratch her furry head and frowned. *We should go back.* Zak never liked to wander far.

Let's keep looking. Alia felt sure the *whump* sound was an asteroid fragment—one of the hissing chunks of rock that barreled in from space sometimes, ever since two big ones collided. She wanted to hold one of those space scraps and feel the heat of its journey, the weight of secrets from places she'd never see.

But maybe this *whump* had been something else—miners working or—

What's that? Zak flew over the uneven rocks toward a shadowy something, steaming beyond the outcrop.

Then he stopped.

Alia caught up, and she understood. *It's them. They're here.*

She used the pronoun recklessly. Who were *they*? No one knew. Not the scientists who monitored the signals. Not the watchers posted on lookout. Not the leaders who rallied their citizens to be "ever-watchful, ever-vigilant, ever-searching the stars" for an arrival.

They're here. Alia thought it again.

She was right.

What had thumped to the parched dry land was not a scrap

of asteroid, but the elaborate remains of a spacecraft designed by intelligent beings. They must have been smarter than anyone Alia and Zak knew. The most advanced extended spaceflight prototypes their own scientists could make were still being tested on the other side of the planet.

We need to go. They might be dangerous. Zak backed away.

Let's just look. Alia circled the wreckage. *Its wings are all broken up. No sign of life.*

But two gleaming, dark, metallic pods seemed to have weathered the landing. They were long and sleek but bulged in the center to make room, Alia presumed, for whatever they carried inside. The smaller one was cracked open along a seam. She approached it slowly.

Be careful. Zak reached down to hold Mip, but she broke loose and rushed up to sniff at the pod's contents.

Shiny, flimsy packages spilled from the crack. Alia picked one up. It made a crinkling sound when she moved it.

Put that down, Zak urged. *We have to go. The watchers must have seen this; they must be on their way. We'll be questioned if we're here when they arrive.*

Wait. Alia knew this was more serious than another asteroid remnant. She knew she should leave it to the watchers. But she wasn't ready. If she couldn't hold a still-warm space rock close to her heart, she would probe the insides of this shiny vessel before she turned over its secrets.

Alia pinched the corners of the package and pulled. It snapped open, and dust flew out.

Zak backed away as if those molecules of the alien world might swirl him up in a magical cloud and spirit him back there, away from everything he'd ever known.

Alia wished that could happen to her. She'd followed reports of the space pioneers, exploring first the moons, then one planet and another. *Take me with you next time,* she always thought. *Take me.*

Alia tipped the crinkly package, and some of the stuff tumbled out—dirt-colored and rough, light and crumbly.

I think it's their food.

She was about to reach back into the pod when she felt Mip's damp nose nudging her.

Alia turned—and she heard it. A scrape, and then a creak, coming from the other pod. The larger one.

Watch out! Zak hissed.

But Alia froze, staring. The pod grew quiet. *It's okay. It was probably just settling.*

Then the capsule let out a low hissing sound. *And that—it's probably . . . air escaping or something.* Alia waited, but there were no more creaks or scrapes, only the steady, quiet hiss of breath from another world.

In the distance, another sound rose over the rocks. The unmistakable buzzing of a team of watchers.

Zak heard it, too. *I told you they'd come. Let's go.*

Not yet. They'll be a while. Alia crouched low, pulled out the rest of the food packets, and reached deeper inside the pod.

What's in there?

Something . . . hard and cold. A weapon. It was too large to fit through the crack in the pod, but still smaller than any weapon Alia had ever seen. *It's not very big. That's good, right?*

But Zak's fear filled the air like fog. *Their weapons are probably smaller because they're more advanced. That thing you're grabbing could annihilate all of us.* Zak reached out to pull her away.

Alia pulled back. *Maybe they don't want to annihilate all of us.*

You're being reckless. We need to get out of here!

Not yet. Alia turned toward the second pod, but Zak rushed forward to stand between her and the capsule. *Have you forgotten everything we were taught? It doesn't matter if they're friendly, Alia. They could carry diseases. What if more come and we're overrun? We don't have enough resources to share.*

Alia cast her eyes down. Everything Zak said was true. And yet . . .

I want to know who they are. She turned back to the first pod. Something glossy was snagged on a sharp edge of metal. Alia tugged it from the capsule and stared.

It was a page of images.

Alia's limbs stiffened, and Zak rushed to her side. She could sense his terror, his revulsion. *Now do you see?*

She did. The creatures in the images were grotesque. Their faces were raw and pink, their bodies soft, mushy-looking, and pale as the moons.

Zak made a troubled clicking sound. *Leave that for the watchers. They'll want to study it. Now let's go.*

But before Alia could turn away, the larger pod creaked again. Then it thumped. A quiet keening came from inside.

Alia, come on! Zak was already climbing away over the rocks.

But she couldn't leave. *Something is in there. Alive.* Even with the horrible images fresh in her brain, she couldn't turn away from that wailing. So she took a step forward. What if . . .

Are you crazy? Zak knocked her to the ground.

They're in trouble, Zak. She started to get up, but Zak clutched her leg. *We need to at least try to help.*

It's not safe. They're not from here, Alia!

So you want to leave them to die? She tugged away from him again and scrambled toward the pod.

Zak trembled. *They're dangerous!*

How do you know? Alia paused. *They look different. But what if they're just like us?*

Zak gave her a dark look. *It won't matter.*

Alia thought hard about that. What if the awful-looking things *were* like them? The flight capsules being developed on their own planet would launch with strict orders to colonize any newly discovered planet, no matter what lived there now. And yet . . . if that were her inside that pod, she'd hope someone would choose courage over fear.

The pod thumped again, louder, over and over. Desperate and powerful. Whatever was in there was strong. But Alia took a step toward the pod.

Alia, no!

What if that were one of us, Zak? We have to try.

He pushed in front of her to block her way. *It's too dangerous.*

The distant buzz of watcher wings grew louder; they'd arrive soon. They'd have the equipment, the weapons and tools and research supplies, to deal with this.

The thumping from the pod faded and finally stopped, and the hissing slowed to a *shhhhhh.*

Quieter.

Quieter. Until silence filled the dry landscape with heaviness.

Maybe that was their breathing apparatus. Alia looked at Zak.

Probably. They must have had a tank like the ones our scientists are working on. They'll be able to study this one and learn from it, I bet. He paused. The watchers were just visible in the distance, flying in from three directions. *Come on. It's too late to help. If we leave now, the watchers won't know we were here.*

Okay. Even Mip seemed to be waiting for her, tipping her antennae toward home, but Alia scratched her behind her crown-horn and turned back to the pod.

It was quiet. The crying had stopped. Whatever sustaining gases they'd brought with them had long leaked away. Whatever had been inside was dead or dying. It had to be this way. Alia's heart ached, but she understood her brother's fear. They couldn't risk everything to help strangers from some far-off world.

Who were you? she wondered. *Where did you come from?*

The only clue was a row of symbols scratched into the pod's dark surface.

E

A

R

T

H

Alia folded her wings tight at her sides, bent low, and ran her antenna over the strange symbols. She traced the straight lines and curves.

E A R T H

Was it the name of a faraway planet? Had the creatures inside the pod dreamed of holding star-scraps in their hands? Had they dreamed of meeting her?

Mip tipped her antennae toward home, and Zak sent out another telepathic thought. *Come on, Alia. We have to go.*

Alia knew he was right. She took one last look at the capsule.

Maybe they would come again, Alia thought, as she and Zak scuttled back toward the settlement with Mip trotting beside them.

Maybe next time, things could be different.

Mike Winchell

Things Will Never Be the Same

Dealing with Change

A couple years after my parents divorced, my father married again. Mom was single and getting into the swing of full-time work, so when Dad remarried, my brothers and I moved out of Mom's house and into Dad's with my stepmother and step-siblings. After the move, everything was new. A new family, a new town, a new neighborhood, a new school, a new group of people, a need for new friends, and in general, a new place in the world.

That move was hard for me. I felt out of place, despite the fact that I had this new, big family. It wasn't easy making friends, or starting in a new school. Now that I think back, I realize what was hardest of all: *change*. That's difficult for us as kids. We get used to things being a certain way, and when we find ourselves in a different situation for the first time, we get all mixed up and feel lost.

Author Rita Williams-Garcia shares how growing up in a military family forces kids to always be on the move and change hometowns on a regular basis. Grace Lin shows us how much things can change over time, and how extreme the differences often are from country to country. Karen Cushman reveals how major world events can drastically change families' lives in a split second.

Rita Williams-Garcia

SMALL TREASURES

spent my early years in a high-rise building of a Far Rockaway housing project in Queens, New York, jailed inside my wooden playpen. My father, an army sergeant, was stationed in Korea for most of my first two years while my mother worked days, leaving my sister, brother, and me home with a sitter who wasn't allowed to take us beyond our apartment's front door. My siblings and I made do. Rosalind and Russell had full run of our one-bedroom apartment, and run they did, while wooden alphabet blocks, an occasional picture book, and the constant antics of my brother and sister provided my entertainment.

There was also Stanley, a corpulent roach named for Stan Laurel of Laurel and Hardy comedic slapstick fame, although in retrospect he should have been named for the heftier Oliver Hardy. My eyes followed Stanley without blinking, suspended by his quest to reach the ceiling, a ceiling I imagined with a hole that led to the outside. Once fascinated by an object, any object, I could stare for long periods, as if waiting for the object to do or become something amazing. No matter how faithfully I stared or how high Stanley scaled our wall, he never made it to the escape hole without plummeting behind the sofa.

Eventually, my father returned stateside with orders to relocate to Fort Huachuca, Arizona, where my siblings and I discovered dirt and the great outdoors. We were explorers in a new world, a southwestern *bajada* with miles of lumpy sandscapes and low mountains dotted with patches of desert scrub, pine trees, and cactus. Our first yard consisted of sun-blanched grass, prickly burrs, and plenty of rocks. Familiar sounds of honking cars, sirens, and newspaper boys barking out the arrival of morning and evening editions were replaced with the chatter and calls of crickets, desert fowl, and coyotes. Lizards, horned toads, and snakes were as plentiful as a New York apartment full of "Stanleys." Even with rocks and cactus needles about, Rosalind, Russell, and I fell into our lot as barefoot pirates, digging around—an Easter egg pail and shovel, our tools. Our first and only major find uncovered a dog's burrowed stash—a small bone, a metal shoehorn, and a sock. We might not have found any real treasure, but we had found a place that felt like home, and that was more valuable than any find.

As was the norm for military life, moving was a constant for our family. We were settling into our desert home when my father received new orders to relocate farther west to Fort Ord, California. Our new environment wasn't the desert playground of Fort Huachuca, but there was no lack of the great outdoors. We moved into a yellow stucco house in an enclave of pastel colored houses on Briggs Circle Street, an endless green lawn haven with no fences to separate the houses. We made friends and got into the swing of running across the green from house to house, pressing our noses against screen doors in search of kickball playmates. A good rain would keep us penned inside, but once the sun broke, we were outside, smelling the air rich with the scent of newly mown grass and red brown soil, perfect for dirt-clod bombs for neighborhood games of "combat zone." In the middle of an explosive dirt barrage, I dug into a hunk of dirt and came up with a cat's-eye marble. I sat and stared at my find, its swirl of yellow and blue at its core, while dirt bombs rained down on my head. Finally, I removed myself from the line of fire so I could stare into the cat's-eye in peace. My siblings weren't too pleased with my desertion of the dirt war, and from that point on, I was labeled a "game killer" and a "weirdo."

Rosalind and Russell couldn't divorce me as a sibling and were stuck with me, especially during summer camp, which wasn't divided by age or grade. They were stuck with the "weirdo" sister who wanted to dig around and find some treasure.

At camp, our teen counselors kept us distracted with math games, art projects, and long, "educational" nature hikes. In the mornings we played math games and worked on art projects. By noon we were hiking among "good oak" and poison oak, while identifying leaves, rocks, and animal droppings, but more important, searching for Indian artifacts. After hiking for about an hour, we'd build a campfire for wiener and marshmallow roasts using the twigs that had fallen on the ground as kindling and utensils. As for the educational component, our camp counselors told stories of Indians once native to our own Monterey County. The stories were equal parts ghost stories, California history, Native American cultural "facts," and archaeology. The acorn-flinging oak trees and our crackling fire made compelling set dressing for stories about hunting, baking clay pots, and fishing in streams with obsidian spears. On one of our hikes a camper had actually found a spearhead, which made us all sharp-eyed, eager to find the next flint spearhead or a clay pot fragment on the next hike. Years later, after we'd left Fort Ord, then Seaside, and then Fort Benning for civilian life, Rosalind confessed that our counselors had "peppered" the trail with fake objects. I was older by the time I learned the truth, but it didn't diminish the disappointment of having had the possibility of finding a small and valuable treasure taken away from me. In all my digging around, I never found more than a bone, shoehorn, a sock, a cat's-eye marble, and some acorns, but it was always the possibility of uncovering a great find that kept me digging and hoping.

Rita Williams-Garcia

THE STORY

FINDERS KEEPERS

Tyler Byron knew what he had to do. If he thought about it too long he'd change his mind. What did his mom say? The best way to remove a Band-Aid was to rip it off. He opened his cigar box and took out his prized find. He didn't even unflap its protective flannel cloth to admire the arrowhead's point or haft, nor did he rake through his growing collection of tans, faint greens, pale pinks, and beige beauties for the feel of them. *Just give it to her*, he ordered himself. *Get it over with, already.*

Tyler wasn't careful with a lot of things, but he was careful with his find. He knew it was special. Not because he read the Professor's book, but because he had found it himself. That's what made it special. Still, he kept it wrapped and tucked it inside the pocket of his polo shirt. Now, to get past his mother.

"Okay. Bye, Mom."

Ms. Byron didn't look up once while she finger-scrolled down her tablet's screen, but her lips curled. "Say hi to Jewel for me."

Tyler clearly heard *I told you so* in her singsong. His mother had been there when he said that awful thing that made his only friend cry. It didn't matter that he'd spoken the plain truth when he congratulated Jewel for winning honorable mention: "Nice art project, but Halima's was more interesting and Kim's was hands-down the best." He said this knowing Kim was Jewel's art room rival and summer camp archenemy. Jewel was so angry that Tyler thought she'd throw her clay sculpture at him, and Jewel had a rocket of a pitching arm on her. Still, Tyler refused to "take back the truth," and his mother warned, "Some things are more important than the truth."

Then last night when Ms. Byron found him staring at his wall—a habit that didn't go unnoticed or unteased by his peers—she fanned her hand before his face to jolt him out of the stare. "Where are you going to get another friend like Jewel?" she asked. For reasons Tyler pretended to not care about, he was virtually friendless, if it weren't for his stepbrothers, cousins, and Jewel.

"Okay," Tyler said as he walked to the door.

"And say hello to the professor," which was what she called Jewel's father. Mr. Perry wasn't a full professor yet, but it was his mother's way of mocking him. It wasn't entirely his mother's fault. Mr. Perry was mockable. For whatever reason, their parents didn't like each other, but Tyler and Jewel never let that get in the way of their friendship.

One hundred and eleven steps to the Perry house. About fifty-two when he ran. Today Tyler was feeling very sorry because he was lonely and a little angry because he had to give away something he treasured to make things right. His anger got him across the green rain-soaked lawn that merged their backyards. He leaped over one of the round petunia-filled flower beds that flanked both sides of the brick patio's edge. Including the leap, he counted one hundred and nine steps.

Tyler pressed the button next to the screen door. The bell chimed but no one answered, although he could hear the clatter of dishes. He rang again.

Jewel appeared before the still-closed screen door, her arms crossed and locked over her chest. She was wearing her cool face, which meant they weren't friends. Her hands were soapy.

"What do you want?"

"Still mad?"

She tossed her head to the side.

"Won't you at least come out here?" he pleaded.

"Who is it, Jewel?" asked a deep voice from inside.

It didn't matter that the Byrons and the Perrys had lived across the lawn from each other since Tyler and Jewel were four, when they had both had a mother *and* a father. It didn't matter that Tyler and Mr. Perry shared an interest in finding hidden treasure. Jewel's father always seemed grumpy, and for that reason Tyler was a little afraid of him, whereas his mother was not.

"No one," Jewel answered her father.

"Tell 'No One' you have dishes to wash."

Tyler still asked, "Then can I come in?"

"No," Jewel said. Her arms were crossed and hugged her ribs tightly.

"Then come outside."

She didn't answer.

"Please," he said. "I brought you something."

"Je-WEL . . . ," said the deep voice.

Jewel sighed, dismissing her father's bellow. She opened the screen door. Not an invitation for him to enter, but just enough to receive the peace offering. "What is it?" Jewel asked.

Tyler smiled. This was a good sign. "I'm giving you the best arrowhead from my collection." He took the prize from his breast pocket, unwrapped the flannel cloth, and presented it to her, openhanded.

He watched her lean over for a better look. She looked at him. And then took the arrowhead.

"You mean *this*?" It was going wrong, although Tyler couldn't see why. "*This* is supposed to make everything all right after what you said in front of everybody?"

She seemed angrier at the arrowhead than she was at him, which took Tyler by surprise. She was supposed to make the sound that he made when he found it at the riverbank. She was supposed to make the sound of knowing it was a rare and beautiful thing.

"You could put a string around the haft and wear it like a necklace. But you'd have to be careful because—"

Before he could finish warning her that she could lose the arrowhead if she didn't tie the string just right, Jewel gripped the projectile, lifted her arm, and hurled the arrowhead into the flower bed of petunias like a baseball at a catcher's mitt.

"Hey!" he shouted.

"Stupid rock!" she shouted back. "Stupid rockhead." She stepped away and slammed the screen door.

Tyler ran to the flower bed and fell on the ground. There were at least a million purple and red flowers in the flower bed and his arrowhead was swallowed up somewhere down in that dirt. He snatched off their purple and red trumpet heads, yanking up whole plants, stems, leaves, and roots out of the soil. As if the flowers weren't enough, the flower bed was thick with leaves. Yucky, sticky leaves. He'd wipe his hands later. Tyler yanked and pulled until he could see clear patches of soil. That stupid Jewel had hurled the arrowhead like a missile. The arrowhead had to have sunk into the oozy loose soil, point first. At least she hadn't pitched it far out into the lawn or even worse, against the red brick patio, scratching or chipping it.

Tyler had to be careful. He didn't want to damage the arrowhead—if it wasn't damaged already. But now that she had thrown it away, the arrowhead was once again his. *His.* Why he thought Jewel would treasure it, he didn't know. In his mind, he had apologized and offered his best treasure to boot, even when he hadn't done anything wrong to begin with.

He used his fingers to rake across the near headless flower bed dirt, back and forth, back and forth, and then finally, the tip of his pointer finger made contact with stone. Now was the time to exercise care. He dug around it. Then under it, just as he had the afternoon he got caught in a rain shower at the riverbank.

★ ★ ★

There had been nowhere to run that day to escape the rain, so Tyler had lain down in the dirt and curled himself in a ball, letting the rain pelt him until the storm ended. When he'd pushed himself up, he'd felt a tip of some kind prick on his hand. He knew to dig around the pointy thing with a twig — he had read it in *Alabama Arrowheads and Artifacts*, written by the Professor. They lived in the heart of Alabama, where, according to the Professor's book, Indians had lived thousands of years ago and had left behind a treasure trove of arrowheads and other artifacts. Tyler had uncovered a beauty of an arrowhead that had blackened over time and was brownish near the tip. It flared and curved and was flaked with tiny dents. The best part was the haft was intact on both sides.

All of Tyler's other arrowheads had come from flea markets and museum gift shops. He'd found this one himself. When he'd returned home, soaked and muddied from the rain and delirious from his find, his mother was only concerned with getting him cleaned up and warm, and hadn't heard a single word of his excited rambling, or bothered to look at the arrowhead. When he told the Professor he had made a real find, thanks to his book for junior archaeologists, the Professor, who wasn't in the best mood, had said, "Good for you," and didn't ask to see it. But when Tyler had shown the arrowhead to Jewel, she gasped and said it was a beauty and would make a great necklace. Later, Jewel had shared a secret with Tyler. She'd said the other professors in her father's archaeology department always made cracks about his children's book. That night, Tyler had torn off a piece of his flannel PJs, cut it down to a small square, and wrapped the perfect arrowhead within it, then placed it in his cigar box with his flea market and gift shop arrowheads.

★ ★ ★

"What have you done to my yard?" The Professor glared down at him. "Boy, you are in big trouble. We'll see what your mother has to say about this!"

Tyler stood up. "Jewel threw it in the flowers, but I got it back." Tyler opened his hand wide. The mostly blackened rock stood out against his soil-caked palm.

The Professor went silent the second Tyler's hand opened. He peered closer, and before he could reach or ask, Tyler clamped his fingers around his prize, turned, and ran home.

★ ★ ★

Ms. Byron was still scrolling through her tablet when Tyler pushed open the back door and stomped past her. He didn't want to talk about it, but his mother was right behind him, fussing about his filthy clothes.

"I tried," he said, wanting to leave it at that.

"And?" she asked, and managed to get his polo shirt over his head in one upward pull.

"She nearly destroyed my arrowhead. She threw it in the flower bed, but I got it back."

His mother giggled. "You tried to give Jewel one of your rocks to make up?"

Tyler huffed, opened his hand, and said, "Look." He'd run so fast he hadn't bothered to wrap the arrowhead back in its protective piece of flannel. Forty-three steps.

Like the Professor, his mother became quiet. She looked even closer. "Tyler, baby . . ."

This wasn't good, Tyler thought. She only called him *baby* when he was injured or sick.

"Tyler, this doesn't belong to you."

"I found it."

"I know," she said. "But I don't think this is something you can keep."

The doorbell rang. Ms. Byron said she'd be right back and that "this wasn't over." She left him.

Tyler was too mad to stare at the wall. "Finders keepers," he told himself. "It's a rule."

He heard a tap on his window and felt a shadow.

As if he couldn't be madder. He pulled back the curtain. "What do you want?"

Jewel flapped her arms, a plea to raise the window. He huffed but released the lock and pushed up the window. In spite of himself, he helped pull her inside, as he had always done.

"What do you want?"

"To warn you."

"About what?"

"They're going to take your arrowhead."

"Who? Your dad?"

She nodded. "I heard him talking to the archaeology department. Then he was on the phone with the Native American museum. I think everyone's excited about the arrowhead. That thing is old. Like, ten thousand years old. And it's from the Southeast Indians. That's what my dad says. So it's not yours."

"I found it," Tyler repeated.

"But that doesn't make it yours."

"It's not fair," Tyler said. "Finders keepers."

"But it's the truth," Jewel sang.

"It's mine."

"You were going to give it to me."

"You threw it away."

Jewel shrugged. They said nothing for a while.

"Tyler," Jewel said.

"What?"

"Truth hurts. Doesn't it?"

He slugged her in the shoulder but not hard. They sat and admired the arrowhead, its brownish-blackened curved, dinted body, its perfect haft, and intact point, against the plaid flannel square, until Tyler broke out a video game.

Ms. Byron and the Professor had been talking in the other room for at least three full levels of Gem Finder. That had to be a record, Jewel noted. Tyler agreed.

Their parents' voices neared Tyler's bedroom door. In less than four steps Tyler would have to hand the arrowhead over.

Stupid Band-Aid.

WHAT REALLY HAPPENED

A LONG LINE AT CUSTOMS

Twelve hours on a plane! I couldn't believe I survived it. Of course, I did sleep most of the time. But that was the longest plane ride I'd ever been on—we crossed the ocean! All the way to get to Taiwan, what my parents called their "homeland," even though we all lived in the United States. It's because they were born and grew up in Taiwan, not like my sisters and I who were born in the United States. We were all American. So as much as my parents called it *homeland*, I knew it wouldn't be home to me. In fact, this was my first time to Taiwan. I was really glad that we didn't come often because the twelve-hour plane ride was super boring.

And if that wasn't enough, we had to wait through a long, long line for something called "customs," too. I don't know why we had to stand in such a long line.

It felt like the line went on forever. Ki-Ki, my younger sister, had already given up standing and was sitting on her suitcase and making Dad pull her. I don't know what took them so long, I felt like all they had to do was stamp passports. But when I complained, Mom just laughed.

Dad laughed, too, and from the way they were laughing, we knew there was joke that they hadn't told us. We begged to know what was so funny until, finally, Mom told us this story:"When Dad and I left Taiwan, I packed very carefully. I wasn't sure what they would have in America. Would they have rice? How cold would it be? Aunts, uncles, relatives from all over came to wish me a good journey—each bringing me a good-bye gift that they made me promise to bring. Every corner of my giant suitcase was stuffed and jammed with everything anyone thought I might need in the faraway place called the United States of America.

"When we finally left, Dad and I had to go through customs, but the line was much, much longer. I was so nervous. As well as stamping papers, the official was opening and checking everyone's luggage, too. I didn't know that was going to happen! With the long line of people watching and waiting, the official opened each person's suitcase and inspected every item inside.

"When it was my turn, the official carefully read my papers, rechecking all the signatures and stamps. Then, he opened my suitcase. He took out all the clothing, squeezing the rolls of socks and shaking my books.

"Then, he opened my small rice cooker and lifted out a roll of toilet paper. He looked at me like he couldn't believe it, and

I heard snickers and laughter from the line behind me. I was so embarrassed. My grandmother had put that it in. She had been afraid that there would be no toilet paper in that strange land of America. Even though I had told her there would be, she wanted me to take a roll 'just in case.' I had agreed, a little bit because deep down I really wasn't sure. But now the official was holding it in his hands suspiciously. He squeezed it and even unrolled it a little until he was finally satisfied that it was simply just a roll of toilet paper.

"He looked at me again, gave a little laugh, and shook his head. By this time, the crowd behind us was laughing loudly. Everyone thought I was a strange girl, bringing toilet paper half-way around the world!"

When Mom finished her story, we couldn't help laughing, too. But even though it was funny, I couldn't help wondering why the officials were so careful. Mom told us that the officials were making sure she wasn't smuggling stolen goods or wasn't a spy.

That surprised me. Spies? Was Mom joking? That sounded like something from a movie. But I didn't have time to think about it because it was finally our turn to go through customs. The uniformed man asked Dad some questions in Chinese, as I watched with big eyes. Would he think we were spies? Would he look at Mom's jewelry to see if it was stolen? But all he did was stamp our passports like everyone else's and then motion us through.

I breathed a sigh of relief. That had been pretty easy. Things were a lot different now in Taiwan. What other things had changed? I didn't know, but I couldn't wait to see more of it!

THE JADE RING

I was packing when Big Uncle knocked on my door.

"You're leaving for America tomorrow," he said.

I nodded even though it wasn't a question. The whole family—aunts, uncles, even the family dogs—knew that tomorrow morning I was leaving on an airplane to the United States, one of only a handful of people to do so in our family. To most of the people in our town, America was an exotic land—something that was only seen on television or read about in newspapers. But I was the only student in all of Taiwan to be chosen for the scholarship to the Bramwood School in Massachusetts, and no one would let me give that up, even though most of them hadn't even heard of Bramwood, Massachusetts, before.

"I want you to take this," he said, handing me a green ring.

I almost dropped it. The ring was jade, such a pure, vivid green that it was almost glowing. It was smooth and glossy with the fineness of silk. And as it lay in my hand, I could almost feel it vibrating with life. There was no mistaking it. This was Great-Grandmother's jade ring.

"I thought this ring was . . . ," I stuttered, "I thought Grandmother gave this ring to the governor."

Big Uncle scowled, and I regretted reminding him of his past and of the governor who had wrongfully jailed him. Grandmother had not given the ring as a gift, for justice was always decided by which party could offer the larger bribe.

"I took it back," he said.

I looked at him with wide eyes and his head rose defiantly.

"That ring has been in our family for over one hundred years," he said, and suddenly his face seemed to shed its tired and worn mask, for his eyes flashed like lightning in a storm. "It was honored and treasured by our ancestors. It was not meant to be just another trinket to adorn a cheap girlfriend of our corrupt governor. I've only taken back what was ours and should never have been lost."

"Won't they be looking for it?" I asked, my thoughts going around and around like the small green circle in my hand.

"You will be flying over the ocean by the time they notice its disappearance," he said, "and you will not be suspected."

"B-but . . . ," I stuttered again, "there's customs agents and . . ."

"Zhenni," he said to me, suddenly quite kind, "don't be nervous. I wouldn't give it to you if I thought you would get in trouble."

I nodded, and stroked the ring, feeling again the smoothness and strength of the stone. Big Uncle scanned my mess of unpacked things strewn on the floor and picked out a small silk pouch.

"Is this your other jewelry?" he asked. As I nodded, he opened it and a tangle of necklaces spilled into his hand. "Put the ring in here."

I did as he told me, but I couldn't help feeling as if the ring looked like a crane among chickens, set against my cheap glass beads and fake gold pins. "Won't it seem kind of obvious there?" I asked.

Big Uncle said nothing, but instead picked up a roll of toilet paper.

"Were you going to bring this?" he asked with a grin.

I snickered.

"Grandma gave it to me," I said. "She thought I should bring it, just in case America didn't have any toilet paper."

I decided not to add that I had been worried about that, too.

Big Uncle again scanned my unpacked objects and then picked up the small rice cooker. He opened it, put the toilet paper inside, and then closed the lid. Then he handed me the rice cooker.

"Just make sure you pack this, too," he said. "Everything is going to be just fine."

★ ★ ★

Everything is going to be just fine. Those were the words I kept repeating to myself over and over again as I left for the next morning for the airport. In some ways, I was glad that I was so nervous about having the ring. Worrying about it kept me from thinking about the fact that I was leaving my home and family on the other side of the world.

So in the dark of morning, after a rushed, hushed, and

tearful good-bye, I found myself alone in a huge crowded room of the airport. Customs, I thought, reminding myself of the steps I had to take. Before I could leave Taiwan, the customs officer had to check me. And my suitcase.

I joined the long line that snaked back and forth across the room, clutching my papers and dragging my suitcase. The line moved slowly, which was good because I could only push my heavy suitcase an inch or so at a time.

I thought about the jade ring in my giant suitcase. That green circle would probably barely fit my little finger. How odd that something so small could be worth so much. When Grandma heard Big Uncle had been arrested, did she hesitate to get the ring? Or had she gone straight to the closet, straight to the small box hidden on the top shelf to get it—knowing that only the most valuable item would ensure Big Uncle's freedom? And after she had died, when Big Uncle went through her things and found the empty box, was that when he knew the price of his freedom? No one would've told him, but they wouldn't have had to. Everyone knew the governor's finest possessions, from the golden carp in his fishpond to his ivory chopsticks, had been "gifts" from unlucky families.

Even though I felt lost in the forest of people in the room, I was suddenly glad I had the ring. I remembered how the small ring, warm in my palm, had felt like a precious quail egg, and not only was I glad that I was taking the ring but I also knew I wanted to take it. It deserved to be away—far away—from clutching fingers that had sullied it with greed. We would both have a new home in the United States of America.

First, however, we had to get there. I was finally close enough to see the end of the line, and I suddenly felt as if I were just being put in a hot oven. At the end of the line, there was a uniformed man checking everyone's papers and *going through everyone's suitcases*!

What would happen when they saw the ring in my suitcase? Would they know it was stolen? Maybe I could pretend I didn't know it was stolen. Would that even matter? And would they still take it away? Maybe the official won't notice it among the rest of my jewelry, I thought faintly. I watched as the uniformed man checked the suitcase lining of the old woman in front of me. He opened her bag of rice and stuck his hand deep in the bag, watching closely as the grains fells from his fingers. I gulped.

When the old woman went through the doors, he beckoned toward me. His dark-blue uniform was the same color of the sky when I had said good-bye to my parents, but his face and eyes were dull. His skin seemed to hang from his face like an opera mask destined never to smile. I watched as he leafed through my papers, comparing me to my photo with a tired glare. When he finished with the papers, he nodded toward my suitcase, which I had to shove with all my might to get to him.

He sighed as he looked at my stuffed suitcase, the layer upon layer of clothes combined with books and bags of tea crammed into shoes. He began with all the clothing, turning my pants pockets inside out and squeezing the rolls of socks. Then he shook my books open to make sure nothing was secreted between the pages. He took out the bag of preserved plums inside the teapot and smelled them. Then, he opened the rice cooker.

I heard the snickers behind me as he held up the roll of toilet paper. I felt as if someone had lit my clothes on fire. Why had Big Uncle told me to bring that toilet paper? Now, the official was going to pay extra attention to me. I clasped my hands tightly together, fighting the urge to cover my face.

The official eyed the toilet paper with suspicion. He squeezed it and unrolled a long length of it, examining the paper fibers. Finally, he looked at me.

"You are bringing toilet paper halfway around the world?" he said, as if his incredulous disbelief forced words out of him.

I could only nod. The officer shook his head in annoyance and rolled his eyes at my suitcase. I could see that he thought if I packed toilet paper, then it must just be full of nonsense articles. Disgusted, he waved his hands at me to leave — wanting to be rid of me as soon as possible.

He hadn't even opened my jewelry bag.

As I collected my things, I heard waves of muffled laughter roll through the line. I knew they were all laughing at me, but I didn't care. As I felt the ring through the cloth of the bag, I knew why Big Uncle had me bring the roll of toilet paper. *Everything is going to be just fine,* he had said. And it was. The jade ring and I were going to the United States of America!

Karen Cushman

MUDFLATS AND OCTOPUSES

My husband, Philip, grew up with sand in his hair and his feet in the waters of Mission Bay, San Diego. It was not the Mission Bay of today, with hotels, golf courses, and SeaWorld, but South Mission, a sandbar that stretched like a finger into the water, the tidal marsh called Mission Bay on one side and the Pacific Ocean on the other.

Phil's father suffered from severe asthma, and in 1950 his doctor recommended a move to the clean, fresh air of the beach. The family chose Mission Bay. For many years I have heard Philip's stories about their small house on the bay, long before the bay was dredged and Mission Bay became a famous resort. The warm bay water lapped at the sand when the tide was in. There was swimming and surfing and volleyball on the beach. He never wore shoes from June until September, and his feet grew callused and summer wide.

Phil would row his small boat out where the reeds and grass grew tall and read comic books until his nose was sunburned and his empty stomach growled. He watched seals tumble in the water and fished for perch and halibut, although more often his hook brought up sand sharks and stingrays, which flopped in the bottom of the leaky boat.

Most intriguing to me as I listened were descriptions of the vast mudflats—stinking, slippery, and mysterious—which appeared like magic when the tide was out. The mud was pocked with pickleweed and eelgrass. Shoals and small islands, home to colonies of mussels and sand dollars standing on end in soldier-like rows, were revealed. The mudflats teemed with insects and small crustaceans, which drew curlews, sandpipers, and plovers, who poked in the mud for their dinner.

Early in the morning, Phil said, Portuguese fishermen would be out catching the octopuses whose hiding holes the ebbing tide had uncovered. The octopuses buried themselves in the mud. Fishermen filled squeeze bottles with bleach and squirted it into holes. The octopuses slithered out to avoid the bleach, whereupon fisherman would grab them and bite right in the nerve center between their eyes. The bite didn't kill an octopus but paralyzed it; it stayed fresher that way. Slip and slide, bleach and a quick bite—the image stayed in my mind. I could almost see it all and smell the bleach, the salt, the fish. Was it true? Did Phil remember it correctly? Intrigued, I investigated further.

Octopuses do not swim in schools. In fact, they live alone and spend most of their time hiding in dens, which makes them rather difficult to catch in large numbers. So in most places octopuses are captured individually. They are highly intelligent creatures, but their inquisitive nature lets fisherman entrap them using simple clay jars placed deep in the water. An octopus peeks in looking for food or a good nesting or mating area and can't slither out. The fisherman then merely pulls out the pot and catches the octopus.

The fishermen of Mission Bay did not need to use clay pots. The two-spotted octopus common in the waters around San Diego is nocturnal. The muddy bottom of the bay provided easy octopus dens, and the ebbing tide left them uncovered, easy to see by fishermen who got there early and caught them just the way Phil told me.

This has all been changed now. In the late 1940s, dredging and filling operations began converting the marsh into what today is Mission Bay Park. Twenty-five million cubic yards of sand and silt were dredged to create the varied land forms of the park, which now is almost entirely man-made. Five million visitors pour into the area each year. Sailboats, Jet Skis, and water-skiers have replaced rowboats, pickleweed, and octopus fishermen.

Phil's little house is gone now. The mudflats are just the bottom of the bay, and the octopus fishermen have moved on to other sites or other jobs. I wish I could have seen it the way it was, but we will always have the stories.

Karen Cushman

THE STORY

CHANGE AND MILLIE MCGONIGAL

Mission Beach, San Diego, 1941

Jorge lifted the slimy creature to his lips and bit it right between the eyes.

I shuddered as I watched. "Doesn't that taste muddy and disgusting?"

"Nah," he said, wiping mud from his mouth. "Only salty. This way they don't die but only sleep, stay fresh." He threw the octopus into a bucket and slipped through the mud-flats to another hole in the muck. He filled a baster from a mud-spattered Clorox bottle and squirted it into the hole. When the occupant slithered to the surface, Jorge pulled it out and bit it, too. "You want? Makes good stew."

I shook my head. I preferred fish that came in cans and was mixed with mayo and chopped celery.

With my bare feet I drew my name in the mud—*Mildred McGonigal*, embellished with whorls and squiggles—as I did every Sunday morning when the tide was out. I liked to do the same things in the same way, and on Sundays it was me and the mud and the bay.

But changes were coming. Only three weeks, and there would be a new year. 1942. Ye gods and little fishes. Change. And next year would be my last in junior high. More change. It seemed to me change brought nothing but trouble — the Depression brought change and my father lost his store, Hitler brought change to Europe and now the radio and my ears were filled with war talk, and since my grandmother Nana got a job checking out books at the library, I hardly got to see her. Couldn't change wait until I was ready?

It was an early morning in December but the sky held the promise of sunshine. The air was rich with the smell of fish, spoilage, and rotten eggs. I breathed deeply of the familiar odor. Gulls screeched overhead. Sandpipers marched their stiff, long-legged march up and back, poking in the mud for worms and snails and tiny crabs. Dragonflies picked off the mosquitoes and fleas that were swarming over the sand and over my feet.

I waved good-bye to Jorge and pulled our battered rowboat over the mud, out to where there was enough water to float in. I climbed in with my toast and jelly and the newest Little House book from the library and rowed myself to the middle. There was jelly on my hands and my face and my book, but it was worth it, and I lay back in luxury. My nana's jelly, made from her own berries, tasted like summer in my mouth.

A splash sounded and a face popped up. The face wore goggles filled with water but I recognized the yellow hair and red, peeling nose of Ricky Bowman, my archenemy. Superman had Lex Luthor; Captain America had the Red Skull; I had Ricky Bowman.

"Well, cut off my legs and call me Shorty, if it ain't Mil-dreadful, the pride of the McGargles."

"Hello, Icky. Let go of my boat and go drown yourself."

"My brother Wendell says the Nazis have invented a secret invincible weapon and will be here before Christmas. That scare you, Mil-dreadful?" he asked with a splash.

"Knock it off. You're ruining my book. And that doesn't scare me half as much as your face."

"Might as well get yourself some leather pants and learn to yodel. The Nazis are coming. *Jawohl, jawohl, heil Hitler!*" Splash. "Be seein' ya." With another splash he was gone.

"Not if I see you first," I muttered.

The morning was spoiled. Icky Bowman. What a pill. I dragged the boat back to the beach. The mud of the flats felt soft and cool on my bare feet. I wiggled my feet so the mud squidged between my toes. I began to march in place, sinking lower and lower until I was in cool mud well past my ankles. Then I wiggled and wriggled my legs until the mud gave me up and I strode off, legs all black and gooey, heading for home, past the tavern and the grocery store and Spider Grossman's tattoo parlor. Every Sunday. I liked to do the same things in the same way. It made me feel warm and cozy, like I was wrapped in a towel freshly dried by the sun and smelling of soap.

"Millie, is that you?" my mother called as I entered. *Who*

else? I thought. Was she expecting Clark Gable to come and take her away from this overcrowded cottage and ungrateful family and sweep her off to Hollywood?

"I saw Daddy with Lily and Pete on their way to the amusement park, so I guess it would have to be me." Baseball blared from the radio, but I leaned over and turned the dial. Glenn Miller, "Chattanoogo Choo Choo." The most! I jitterbugged around the kitchen a while, then threw myself down on a kitchen chair and began scratching the dried mud off my leg with a fork.

"Mildred McGonigal, if you can't act like a lady, at least try and act like a human being." My mother shoved her stack of recipe cards away and took a slurp of her coffee. "I sent your father and the little ones out so we could talk," she said. She lit a cigarette and blew a great puff of smoke into the air. "You know my mother has taken a job. It will mean some changes for us." *Changes*, that nasty word again. I feared this meant no good for me. My nana was smaller than me but twice as strong and three times as tough. She lived in North Park, on Utah Street, down the block from where baseball star Ted Williams, the Splendid Splinter, grew up. So what would her job have to do with us? And specifically, me?

"Cousin Nadine can no longer be left alone while Nan is at work." Mom stubbed her cigarette out in her saucer after a few more puffs. "She will have to come here and live with us."

Gadzooks! Cousin Nadine was some sort of third or fourth cousin who lived with Nana and was nothing but trouble. She had yellow false teeth and dyed black hair. And she was a stink machine! Powerful-smelling gas exploded from her top and her bottom. Hook her up and she could power all the stoves in San Diego! "You can't mean that. We are already crowded in here. Where will she sleep? And eat? And—"

I knew. I knew why my mother and I were having this special little talk. There were only two bedrooms in this cottage, and sure as shootin' Cousin Nadine wouldn't be bunking with my parents.

"She'll move in with you and Lily, and Pete will use the sofa."

"But—"

"I know. I know what you're going to say. She belches and passes gas, dribbles and drools. She loses her glasses and her teeth and repeats herself over and over. But she's family and she needs us and we will be there for her. And that's it."

"But I—"

"That's enough out of you," she said. "This is a family, not a democracy." As if that hadn't been obvious every day of my life. She changed the radio station back to the baseball game. I stomped into the bedroom, but quietly so as not to get in too much trouble.

I stuck my head out the window and sniffed deeply of the reek of the mudflats. Other people called it stink. To me it was perfume, the fragrance of my life, my home, and it comforted me.

Gadzooks. Cousin Nadine. Another change, and I could not

think of anything worse. I took another deep breath. I needed all the comfort I could get.

"Millie!" My mother screamed from the other room. My mother? Raising her voice? This might not have seemed like such a big deal to most people, but my mother graduated from the school of No Arguing or Whining where she majored in Never Raise Your Voice and Act Like a Lady.

"Millie!!!" Gadzooks. Don't flip your wig, Mama.

She pushed my door open and grabbed my arm. "Run and find your father and the children. Now, Millie! Now!"

"What for? Why me?" I was getting a good whine up when she grabbed me by the shoulders and shook.

"The radio," she said. "The Japanese." She was breathing heavily. "Hawaii. Bombs. Get your father now!"

I went. All I knew of Hawaii was pineapples and grass skirts, but it was near us, not far away like Germany and France. Did Japanese bombs mean war was heading here? My throat was dry and my heart flopped like a fish as I ran toward the amusement park. I met my pop and the kids coming home.

"Bombs," I said through pants and wheezes. "Hawaii. Bombs."

He picked Lily up and ran, Pete and me following.

We spent the rest of that Sunday huddled around the radio. There wasn't much news really, just the same stories of bombs and fires and sunken ships. I knew this would mean whopping big changes. *More* changes. Always more. I chewed on my cuticles until they bled.

That night we were awakened by the noise of airplanes flying near us, probably from the Naval Air Station on North Island, but the sound was frightening—warlike and ominous.

Lily and Pete climbed into my bed. "We're afraid," said Lily.

"Are those Japanese planes?" Pete asked. "Are they going to bomb us?"

"Can we sleep with you?" they asked together.

"Okay, okay, but you, Lily, have to promise not to wet the bed. And Pete, no hogging the covers." We snuggled in and Lily stuck her thumb in her mouth. "You remember Captain Midnight and his Secret Squadron from the radio?" I asked. "They fly around fighting criminals and spies, remember? That's who you hear up there. Not the Japanese; Captain Midnight. Whoosh. Swoop. There he is again. After the bad guys. Keeping us safe."

I knew better and felt a little shiver of fright at the sound of planes going to war, and Pete still looked a little suspicious, but Lily totally bought it. We made up stories about Captain Midnight and Superman, Dick Tracy, and even the Lone Ranger, fighting the Japanese. Comforted a little, we fell asleep.

Next day, we listened as the president declared war on Japan. Seemed to me Japan had already done that with their bombs.

As days went on, no Japanese planes attacked Mission Beach, but there were more changes. Holy cow, growing up was hard enough without the world changing so fast, too. Because of rumors about Japanese submarines in San Diego

Harbor, my mother insisted we move away from the beach and into town where we would live at Nana's house. My mother got a job on the assembly line at Consolidated Aircraft. For the duration of the war, she said, she would be making airplanes instead of dinner. Nana bought eye protectors and signed up at the Vocational Center to become a welder. My pop had a heart murmur so the army would not take him. Instead, he got a job as a clerk at the Navy Exchange, so it was almost like he got his store back. I could see in their tired faces the fear and uncertainty that change was bringing.

By the end of the month, the movers had come and we were squeezed into Nana's house. I was in charge of Lily and Pete and Cousin Nadine before and after school. Pete and I started a scrap paper drive and pulled his red Radio Flyer wagon through the streets of North Park, picking up papers.

During Christmas vacation I visited the beach once more. I knew I wouldn't be going very often. From Nana's house to the beach meant a streetcar, the #16 bus, a lot of walking, and more nickels than I had. Under a winter gray sky, I walked over to the bay to say good-bye. The tide was up so Jorge and the others were not there. Our empty rowboat bobbed sadly in the shallow water. A couple of little kids had built a sand castle and were in the process of gleefully bombing it with mud balls and rocks.

Crossing Mission Boulevard, heading for the ocean side, I passed Spider Grossman looking spiffy in his navy uniform with white hat cocked just so. When did he get so dreamy? I saluted him and he saluted back with a wink.

I stood a long while and watched waves come in and go out again. In and out. In and out, changing the shape of the sand. In and out. In and out. Change, I realized, occurred whether or not I was ready for it, and I had to do my best to adapt with a minimum of fuss. I still didn't have to like it, though.

Ricky Bowman barreled down the boardwalk on his bicycle, ringing the bell. Wouldn't you know Icky would be the last memory I would have of the beach? But surely the coming of the war had changed things. We were allies, joined in a war against far worse archenemies than each other, weren't we? Would we be friends now?

"If it ain't Mil-dreadful, ugly as ever." He rolled over my foot with another jingle of his bell.

Some things never change. It was a bit of comfort, though I would never tell that to Icky Bowman.

Acknowledgments
Mike Winchell

This book is about inspiration, so it's only fitting that I take the time to thank the many people who have served a role in contributing to its creation.

First, I'd like to thank Grosset & Dunlap and the entire Penguin family for being the perfect home for this project. Specifically, my sincerest thanks to my editor, Bonnie Bader, and the lovely Renee Hooker, who have both worked tirelessly to make this book as great as we all knew it could be. Bonnie and Renee, thank you for your initial belief, shared vision, and constant support. I hope I haven't let you down.

Thank you to my agent, Brianne Johnson, who immediately believed in this project when I pitched it to her, despite the fact that it was merely an idea and some author names at that point. Bri, I know you bought in on *me*, too, and I appreciate you always championing my work. I look into my crystal ball and see us sharing many "Post-it Note" accomplishments in the years to come.

To Alyssa Eisner Henkin, for her guidance during a couple trying years. Alyssa, more than anything, you helped me understand the tricky nature of the business. Without your support, I don't think this (or any) book would make it to the shelf.

Thanks to my best writing buddy—and *Been There, Done That* contributor—Tracy Edward Wymer. Your friendship and advice has meant the world to me. And to my fellow Liverpool Warrior John Zeleznik for his presence, Shaun David Hutchinson for "being there" to bounce things off of, and Project Mayhem for helping to flesh out the rough idea that was in my head. Thanks to Stephanie Zerillo for her consistent presence and friendship over the years.

I owe thanks to my Cortland Junior-Senior High School family, especially Team Four for putting up with my reading and writing obsessions, and listening to my many ramblings about the publishing world. To my former students: Ezra Engst-Mansilla (my first reader), the "Coffee Girls" (Sarah Endress and Ally Kruman), and Ariana Cornish and Taylor Warren (no, I didn't forget you two).

Thanks to the Staffords, the best in-laws a guy could ask for. A special note to my mother-in-law, Lydia Stafford, and my late father-in-law, Arthur Stafford, the reason for my son's first name: I know you're looking down on us smiling, Art.

I've long appreciated my brothers, Tim and Jeff, for being there for me. You're both good men, and I hope I don't spoil that trend too much. To another good man, my stepfather, Garry White, who always seems to be there when I need him, usually to fix something in my house that I have just broken.

A sentimental thank you to my mother, Gerrie White, who has always been the rock in my life. Without your constant love, support, and blind belief in me, I would not have accomplished anything. Thank you for everything, Mom.

Most importantly, to my best friend and wife Shelby for . . . well . . . Any other word would not adequately express what you mean to me. And to my children, A.J. and Savannah, my life found meaning when you two were born. Daddy loves you more than anything in the world!

Mike Winchell

Authors

GARY D. SCHMIDT is the author of novels for middle-grade and young-adult readers, including *Lizzie Bright and the Buckminster Boy*, *The Wednesday Wars*, *Okay for Now*, *What Came from the Stars*, and *Orbiting Jupiter*. He teaches writing both at Calvin College and in Hamline University's MFA program in Writing for Children and Young Adults. When not teaching, he's typing on a 1953 Royal back at home in Alto, Michigan. Visit him at www.hmhbooks.com/schmidt.

CAROLINE STARR ROSE spent her childhood in the deserts of Saudi Arabia and New Mexico, camping by the Red Sea in one and eating red chilies in the other. She has taught social studies and English, and worked to instill in her students a passion for books, an enthusiasm for experimenting with words, and a curiosity about the past. Caroline was named a *Publishers Weekly* Flying Start author for her debut novel, *May B.*, which was an ALA/ALSC Notable Children's Book and received two starred reviews. She is also the author of the historical verse novel *Blue Birds* and the picture book *Over in the Wetlands: A Hurricane-on-the-Bayou Story*. Visit her at www.carolinestarrrose.com.

ALAN LAWRENCE SITOMER is a California Teacher of the Year award winner and the founder of the Writer's Success Academy. In addition to having been an inner-city high-school English teacher and a former professor in the Graduate School of Education at Loyola Marymount University, Mr. Sitomer is a nationally renowned keynote speaker who specializes in engaging underperforming students. To date, Mr. Sitomer has authored seventeen books, with works ranging from hard-hitting young-adult novels like *Homeboyz*, *Caged Warrior*, and *Hip-Hop High School* to humorous and warm children's picture books such as *Daddies Do It Different* and *Daddy's Zigzagging Bedtime Story*. Additionally, he is the author of two teacher methodology books and a classroom-curriculum series for secondary English language arts instruction called The Alan Sitomer BookJam. His latest young-adult novel, *Noble Warrior*, has garnered some of the best reviews of his career. Visit him at www.alanlawrencesitomer.com.

CLAIRE LEGRAND used to be a musician until she realized she couldn't stop thinking about the stories in her head. She now writes full-time. Her first novel is *The Cavendish Home for Boys and Girls*, one of the New York Public Library's 100 Titles for Reading and Sharing in 2012. She is also the author of *The Year of Shadows* and *Winterspell*, a young-adult retelling of *The Nutcracker*. She is one of the four authors behind the anthology *The Cabinet of Curiosities*, a Junior Library Guild selection and one of the New York Public Library's

100 Titles for Reading and Sharing in 2014. Visit her at www.claire-legrand.com and at www.enterthecabinet.com.

Born in New York City in 1950, **JULIA ALVAREZ** returned with her parents to their native country, the Dominican Republic, shortly after her birth. Ten years later, the family was forced to flee to the United States because of her father's involvement in a plot to overthrow the dictator Rafael Trujillo. Alvarez has written novels (*How the García Girls Lost Their Accents*, *In the Time of the Butterflies*, *¡Yo!*, *In the Name of Salomé*, *Saving the World*), poetry (*Homecoming*, *The Other Side/El Otro Lado*, *The Woman I Kept to Myself*), nonfiction (*Something to Declare*, *Once Upon a Quinceañera*, *A Wedding in Haiti*), and books for young readers (including the Tía Lola Stories series, *Before We Were Free*, *Finding Miracles*, and *Return to Sender*). Alvarez's awards include the Pura Belpré and Américas Awards. She was awarded the National Medal of Arts by President Obama in 2014. She is currently a writer in residence at Middlebury College. Visit her at www.juliaalvarez.com.

LINDA SUE PARK is the author of several novels and picture books, including the 2002 Newbery Medal winner *A Single Shard* and the *New York Times* Best Seller *A Long Walk to Water*. Her most recent title is *Xander's Panda Party*, a picture book illustrated by Matt Phelan. She has also written two books in Scholastic's multiplatform series *The 39 Clues*. Linda Sue knows very well that she will never be able to read every great book ever written, but she keeps trying anyway. Visit her website at www.lindasuepark.com and follow her on Twitter at @LindaSuePark.

In 2004, **LISA YEE**'s debut novel, *Millicent Min, Girl Genius*, won the first Sid Fleischman Humor Award. Since then, she has written ten more novels, including *Stanford Wong Flunks Big-Time*, *Absolutely Maybe*, and *Bobby vs. Girls (Accidentally)*, plus books for American Girl. Lisa's most recent novel is for teens—*The Kidney Hypothetical: Or How to Ruin Your Life in Seven Days*. Accolades include Thurber House Children's Writer-in-Residence, Fox Sports Network "American in Focus," *Publishers Weekly* Flying Start, and *USA Today* Critic's Top Pick, plus *Washington Post* Book of the Week, *Sports Illustrated Kids'* Hot Summer Read, and NPR Best Book of Summer. Visit Lisa at www.lisayee.com or catch her procrastinating on Facebook.

CHRIS RYLANDER is the author of the acclaimed *Fourth Stall* saga and the Codename Conspiracy series. He loves unevenly diced apples, conversational toasters with infectious laughs, and half-eaten nachos. He lives in Chicago with his wife and a mutant dog. Visit him at www.chrisrylander.com.

DEE GARRETSON writes middle-grade and young-adult fiction, and is delighted to have recently added chapter books to her repertoire. Her first book, *Wildfire Run*, was a Junior

Library Guild selection and has been nominated for seven state awards lists. *Wolf Storm* was a Scholastic Book Club selection and has been nominated for three state awards lists. Her most recent work is a Boxcar Children book called *The Headless Horseman*. Dee lives in Ohio with her husband and two children, all of whom are pressed into service for story brainstorming. Their two cats are part of her Skype team for school and library chats, and often steal the show. She can be contacted at www.deegarretson.com.

NATHAN HALE is the creator of Hazardous Tales, the *New York Times* best-selling series of graphic novels on American history. He is also the Eisner-nominated illustrator of *Rapunzel's Revenge* and its sequel, *Calamity Jack*. He lives in Utah. He maintains an online collection of comics and illustration at www.spacestationnathan.com.

MATTHEW J. KIRBY is the critically acclaimed and award-winning author of the middle-grade novels *The Clockwork Three*, *Icefall*, *The Lost Kingdom*, *Infinity Ring Book 5: Cave of Wonders*, the Quantum League series, and the Dark Gravity Sequence. He was named a *Publishers Weekly* Flying Start, he has won the Edgar Award for Best Juvenile Mystery, the PEN Center USA award for Children's and Young Adult Literature, and the Judy Lopez Memorial Award, and he has been named to the New York Public Library's 100 Titles for Reading and Sharing list, and the ALA Best Fiction for Young

Adults list. He is a former school psychologist and currently lives in Utah with his wife and three stepkids. Visit him at www.matthewjkirby.com/kirbside.

TRACY EDWARD WYMER is the author of *The Color of Bones* and *Soar*, coming in spring 2016. When he's not plowing through the never-ending pile of books on his nightstand, he likes to run, write, watch birds, and root for the Kansas City Royals. A longtime educator, he lives with his family in Los Angeles, California. Visit him at www.tracyedwardwymer.com.

JANE YOLEN, often called "the Hans Christian Andersen of America," is the author of over 350 books, including *Owl Moon*, *The Devil's Arithmetic*, and *How Do Dinosaurs Say Good Night?* The books range from rhymed picture books and baby board books, through middle-grade fiction, poetry collections, and nonfiction, and up to novels and story collections for young adults and adults. A graduate of Smith College, with a master's degree in education from the University of Massachusetts, she teaches workshops, encourages new writers, and lectures around the world. Her books and stories have won an assortment of awards—two Nebulas, a World Fantasy Award, a Caldecott Medal, the SCBWI Golden Kite Award, three Mythopoeic awards, two Christopher Awards, a nomination for the National Book Award, and the National Jewish Book Award, among many others. Six colleges and universities have given her honorary doctorates. Also worthy of note, her Skylark Award—given by

NESFA, the New England Science Fiction Association—set her good coat on fire. If you need to know more about her, visit her website at www.janeyolen.com.

HEIDI E. Y. STEMPLE didn't want to be a writer when she grew up. In fact, after she graduated from college, she became a probation officer in Florida. It wasn't until she was twenty-eight years old that she gave in and joined the family business, publishing her first short story in a book called *Great Writers & Kids Write Spooky Stories*. The great writer was her mom, author Jane Yolen. Since then, she has published almost twenty books, including *Not All Princesses Dress in Pink*, the Unsolved Mystery from History series, and two Fairy Tale Feasts cookbooks, as well as numerous short stories and poems, mostly for children. Heidi lives and works on an old tobacco farm in western Massachusetts. Her website is www.heidieystemple.com.

ADAM REX is the *New York Times* best-selling author and/or illustrator of over twenty books for kids, including *Frankenstein Makes a Sandwich* and the middle-grade novel *The True Meaning of Smekday*, which provided the inspiration for the DreamWorks animated film *Home*. Adam's home is in Tucson, Arizona, with his son and astrophysicist wife. Visit him at www.adamrex.com.

MARGARITA ENGLE is the Cuban American author of many young-adult verse novels about the island, including *The*

Surrender Tree, which received the first Newbery Honor ever awarded to a Latino, and *The Lightning Dreamer*, recipient of the 2014 PEN Center USA award for Children's and Young Adult Literature. Other honors include multiple Pura Belpré and Américas Awards, as well as Jane Addams, International Reading Association, Claudia Lewis, International Latino, and MANA Las Primeras Awards. Books for younger children include *Mountain Dog, Summer Birds, Orangutanka,* and *Drum Dream Girl.* Margarita grew up in Los Angeles, but developed a deep attachment to her mother's homeland during summers with her extended family in Cuba. *Enchanted Air: Two Cultures, Two Wings* is a verse memoir about those Cold War–era childhood visits. Margarita was trained as a botanist and agronomist before becoming a full-time poet and novelist. She lives in central California, where she enjoys hiding in the wilderness to help train her husband's search-and-rescue dogs. Learn more by visiting www.margaritaengle.com.

KATE MESSNER is the author of more than two dozen current and forthcoming books for kids, including the Silver Jaguar Society mysteries and the Marty McGuire and Ranger in Time chapter-book series, picture books like *Over and Under the Snow, Up in the Garden and Down in the Dirt,* and *How to Read a Story,* and novels like *Wake Up Missing and All the Answers.* Her books have been honored with an E.B. White Read Aloud Award and Honor, an SCBWI Golden Kite Award, and two SCBWI Crystal Kite Awards, and her titles have appeared on more than twenty state book-award lists. Kate's books for educators, *Real Revision* and *59 Reasons to Write*, are published by Stenhouse. A former middle-school English teacher, Kate earned National Board Certification in 2006. She lives on Lake Champlain with her family. Find her on Twitter at @KateMessner and at www.katemessner.com.

RITA WILLIAMS-GARCIA is the *New York Times* best-selling author of nine novels for young adults and middle-grade readers. Her most recent titles are *P.S. Be Eleven, One Crazy Summer, Jumped,* and *Gone Crazy in Alabama,* and her short stories and essays have appeared in numerous anthologies. She is a two-time winner of the Coretta Scott King Author Award and a National Book Award Finalist. Her multi-award-winning novel *One Crazy Summer* was also the recipient of the Scott O'Dell Award for Historical Fiction, a Newbery Honor, and the Parents' Choice Award, and has been listed on many state reading lists. She was the 2012 Charlotte Zolotow lecturer and the 2015 Virginia Hamilton lecturer. Ms. Williams-Garcia is on the faculty of the Vermont College of Fine Arts MFA in Writing for Children & Young Adults program, and she resides in Jamaica, Queens, New York. Visit her at www.ritawg.com.

GRACE LIN is the author and illustrator of picture books, early readers, and middle-grade novels. Her first book, *The Ugly Vegetables,* was published in 1999 and was quickly heralded. Grace expanded the boundaries of middle-grade fiction with her Newbery Honor book *Where the Mountain Meets the Moon*, as well as the companion novel, *Starry River of the Sky*. Her early reader Ling & Ting series is well underway; the first installment, *Ling & Ting: Not Exactly the Same!*, was named a *New York Times* Notable Children's Book and a Theodor Seuss Geisel Honor Book. Grace is now at work on another novel as well as a new picture book. Grace lives in Florence, Massachusetts, with her husband and daughter. More information can be found at www.gracelin.com.

KAREN CUSHMAN lives, works, and procrastinates on a misty green island near Seattle, where she is encouraged by her husband and distracted by her cat. She has published eight books since she started writing at age fifty, including the Newbery Medal winner *The Midwife's Apprentice* and *Catherine Called Birdy*, a Newbery Honor book. Karen was born in Chicago, where she enjoyed snow, thunderstorms, and her grandparents. When she moved to Los Angeles at ten, she lost them all. "I missed my dog, my grandparents, and my public library," she says, sentiments that readers of *The Ballad of Lucy Whipple* will recognize. A fortuitous scholarship sent her to Stanford University, where she majored in Greek and English. After marrying Philip in 1969, she went back to school and earned a master's degree in human behavior and another in museum studies. For eleven years she was an adjunct professor of museum studies at John F. Kennedy University in the California Bay

Area before resigning to write full-time. She is now at work on a new book. It took her forty-nine years of preparation to be ready to write. Now she has no plans to stop. Visit her at www.karencushman.com.